A Flight Simulator Odyssey

Charles Gulick

COMPUTE! Books
Greensboro, North Carolina
Radnor, Pennsylvania

Other books by Charles Gulick
Flight Simulator Co-Pilot
Flying Flight Simulator
40 Great Flight Simulator Adventures
40 More Great Flight Simulator Adventures
Runway USA

Other Flight Simulator books from COMPUTE! Books
COMPUTE!'s Flight Simulator Adventures for the Amiga, Atari ST, and Macintosh
Flying on Instruments with Flight Simulator
Learning to Fly with Flight Simulator
Realistic Commerical Flying with Flight Simulator

Copyright 1989, COMPUTE! Publications, Inc. All rights reserved.

Edited by Stephen Levy
Cover design by Anthony Jacobson

Printed in the United States of America

10 9 8 7 6 5 4 3 2 1

Library of Congress Cataloging-in-Publication Data
Gulick, Charles.
    A flight simulator Odyssey/Charles Gulick.
        p.   cm.
    Includes index.
    ISBN 0-87455-177-3
    1. Flight simulators.   2. Airplanes—Piloting—Data processing.
    I. Title.
    TL712.5.G852   1989
    629.132'52'078—dc19   88-39584
                                                      CIP

COMPUTE! Publications, Inc., Post Office Box 5406, Greensboro, NC 27403, (919) 275-9809, is a Capital Cities/ABC, Inc. company and is not associated with any manufacturer of personal computers. Amiga is trademark of Commodore-Amiga, Inc. Atari ST is a trademark of Atari Corporation. Commodore 64 is a trademark of Commodore Electronics Limited. *Flight Simulator* is a registered trademark of SubLogic Corporation licenced to Microsoft Corporation. IBM is a registered trademark of International Business Machines. Macintosh is a trademark of Apple Computer, Inc. Microsoft and MS-DOS are registered trademarks of Microsoft Corporation.

Contents

Contents

Contents

Contents

Preface

A *Flight Simulator Odyssey* will take you and your airplane to more than 120 choice locations in today's greatly enhanced simulator world, ready to experience the realism, excitement, and challenge the world has to offer. You'll sightsee virtually every major landmark . . . view the most scenic vistas . . . execute more than three dozen straight-in and pattern airport approaches . . . visit numerous historic sites and learn something about them . . . relive major events on the scene, from Washington crossing the Delaware to the Wright brothers at Kitty Hawk to the Johnstown flood to the invasion of Normandy . . . meet people and legends like P.T. Barnum, Howard Hughes, Charles Lindbergh, Paul Bunyan, and many more . . . fly "contact" along rivers like the Rappahannock and St. Johns in the U.S. to the Seine in France, the Thames in England, and the Rhine in Germany.

You'll never want for fun or challenge as you tackle more than 30 "wild times and shenanigans" scenarios, from impromptu landings that call for all your skills to flights demanding your most artful dodging techniques to the fascinating new "glider chase" sport (a thrill-a-minute game in itself) introduced by the author.

For those new to *Flight Simulator* we'll first take quick looks at some major landmarks and features in the New York, Chicago, Los Angeles, Seattle, and San Francisco Bay areas (even old-timers may find these interesting due to the fresh perspectives involved). Then we'll be off to explore in-depth the upgraded scenes and detail of the latest Scenery Disks: 7, 11, and Western European Tour (14).

As you fly, you'll learn something about the physical world below you. You'll also add to your flying skills, because many, if not all, the scenarios involve application of essential aircraft control techniques—some, indeed, calling for your very sharpest judgment. But the emphasis in this book is on the pleasure, sights, and sheer adventure of flying, rather than on instruction. However, if you are new to the idea of flying, there's a "Basic Flying Guide," Appendix A.

Inevitably, some instructional comments will appear in the course of the flights we make in this book. (The author asks the forbearance of advanced pilots in regard to these comments; they are intended for those less skilled.)

CHAPTER ONE
The Flight Plan

Flight Simulator Odyssey is a series of more than 120 flights of various lengths. It has been written for both the beginning and experienced *Flight Simulator* pilot. The *Odyssey* assumes that you know how to fly the *Simulator*. If you are new to the *Simulator* or if you just want a refresher course in *Flight Simulator* flying, read Appendix A, "Basic Flying Guide."

En Route Starter

You'll make a number of point-to-point flights in *Odyssey*, taking off from some of *Flight Simulator's* most colorful airports, flying scenic routes, and landing at U.S., European, and other airports you may never have seen. But long flights will be relatively infrequent.

A majority of the scenarios will place you aloft, in a selected position, and on a specific compass heading. Using this technique, I can acquaint you with more of the simulator world, in a shorter span of time, and from the best vantage points.

For these en route scenarios you'll need to recall a prior en route situation (we'll create and save a *starter* at the outset). This situation will have you straight and level at a medium speed of 80–90 KIAS (Knots Indicated AirSpeed) in your Cessna or Piper, at a nominal altitude of 1500 feet. This is the ideal sightseeing speed, and also the ideal airport approach speed for these aircraft. If you're flying Cessna, your gear will be down (the Piper has fixed landing gear).

For scenarios that begin with the plane in flight, you'll first recall either the original en route starter situation, or any situation derived from it (any flight that starts in the air). I'll then give you the North and East parameters, the desired altitude and heading and, when they matter, the NAV frequency and OBS (Omni-Bearing Selecter) setting and any other pertinent conditions.

If you're flying an earlier version of *Flight Simulator* that lets you enter airspeed, elevator position, heading, and so forth, I'll set you up in the Editor with the parameters for the en route configuration in the course of the first flight.

If you're flying a later version of *Flight Simulator,* one that doesn't accommodate direct entry of heading, airspeed, control-surface parameters, and so on, you'll need to fly the airplane into en route configuration and then save that mode. Thereafter, for an en route scenario, you'll enter the coordinates and altitude and then SLEW to the given heading. Since SLEWing resets the elevator to its default position, destroying whatever trim you had in place, in the first flight I'll show Amiga and Atari ST pilots an easy way to reset your en route trim.

If you're flying the Macintosh version, you are not blessed with a keyboard or keypad yoke. Unfortunately (to my mind, anyway), you must fly with the mouse. Pay close attention to the Controlling Airspeed section below, and to relevant information in the "Basic Flying Guide" (Appendix A). In the course of the en route starter flight, you'll refer to these as you work to get your Cessna into the en route configuration.

Now before that first flight, let's start with a few ground rules.

Saving Situations

At least one scenario (one having the en route parameters) should be saved on disk and should be available when you fly *Odyssey;* otherwise you'll have to re-create the en route configuration before you can start flying. It will also save time if you have an on-the-ground scenario ready for recall, too (for flights that begin at an airport or other ground location). Beyond that, feel free, of course, to save anything else if the mood strikes you. If your position on an airport appeals to you, save it for future use (you never know when you might decide to fly out of there). If the scenery at some stage of a flight pleases you, save the situation to recall later for flights on your own. If a flight is inbound for a landing, you may want to save it at the outset or at the final approach stage, so you can recall it for practice purposes. Or maybe you'll want to save every flight you make in *Odyssey*—you're the boss.

What You Should Know

This book expects you know how to handle your airplane and the various features of your version of *Flight Simulator* reasonably well. It's hoped that you can fly your aircraft at different speeds, specifically at maximum cruise (highest), approach (medium), and slowflight (final approach/landing) speeds. An approach speed in the range of 80–90 KIAS (gear down) may be regarded as both medium and slow flight speed for the purposes of this book. If the idea of basic and inflight speed variations is unfamiliar to you, see Controlling Airspeed later in this section, as well as the "Basic Flying Guide."

You should know how to use the Editor or Menu afforded by your program to set any and all parameters and to SLEW. If you don't, consult your program manual.

Not Machine Specific

Some flights will involve the use of the NAV 1 radio and its associated OBS to fly to or from VOR stations (OMNIs) on selected radials. Complete understanding of VOR navigation is not essential, since you will usually be guided by the text in the course of the flight. But you'll have to be able to tune the NAV radio to specific frequencies and "crank in" (set) a given course (radial) on the OBS. Again, if need be, consult your program manual. The *Basic Flying Guide* also covers VOR navigation, though briefly.

Because *A Flight Simulator Odyssey* is not machine- or version-specific, reference to various control, viewing, and other keys is avoided in the book. Further, if you have a choice of aircraft in your program version, you may, of course, fly the book's point-to-point itineraries in any plane you select. Most of the short-flight scenarios, however, will be more satisfying if you're in a propeller-driven aircraft, and at the en route speed described earlier. The author will consistently fly a Cessna, so pilots without the luxury of a choice of planes can "keep up," or at least not get too far behind.

Some simulator versions offer only fixed (nonretractable) gear aircraft. Thus an occasional reference in the book to "get the gear up" or "drop your gear" is obviously only intended for pilots who have retractable gear. The author will use retractable gear only in those longer flights when a maximum-cruise speed mode is called for. In those cases, maximum cruise will be suggested in the relevant chapter, and pilots with fixed-gear aircraft should simply fly them at their best design speed.

Similarly, some versions do not offer from-the-ground (tower) or spot-plane views of the aircraft. For versions that do, such views will be suggested in the book where appropriate. Tower NORTH, EAST and ALT parameters will be provided for a number of flights for those pilots who have the means to use them.

Parameters and SLEWing

Some of the more recent versions of *Flight Simulator* accommodate precise NORTH and EAST positioning, for example N16447.487. If you're flying an earlier version, you can't enter the fractional value. The resultant difference in positioning (particularly on the ground) can be considerable. To get around this problem, both short-form and long-form parameters will sometimes be given when the aircraft is on the ground, with the long-form parameters in parentheses, for example N16447 (16447.487). This enables you to position your aircraft optimally for your version. On occasion, for maximum viewing or other advantage, the compass heading for the later versions will also be different (again, only when the aircraft is on the ground). In these cases the optimal heading for those versions will be in parentheses, for example, Heading: 090 (083).

   In some versions, as mentioned earlier, the compass heading can be set directly in the Editor; in others (later versions) you must turn the aircraft (if on the ground) or SLEW to the stated heading. In the latter case, remember that SLEWing resets the elevator to the default trim, so you must retrim for the aircraft you are flying in order to obtain the expected takeoff performance or, given an en route scenario, the expected flight characteristics when you unpause.

Environmental Factors

You will not find surface winds, winds aloft, or turbulence parameters in this book. They're avoided for several reasons: to make the flights easier for less-experienced pilots who have enough to do just trying to hold a heading, let alone battling cross-winds and bumpy air; to establish uniform flying and viewing conditions for all pilots, regardless of version or computer type; and finally, if you choose to save the airport situations provided in some chapters as basic situations, you can later fly on your own from those airports, in any direction, under any wind, weather, time-of-day, or other conditions you elect to set.

If you like more of a challenge in your flying, you are of course free to set surface and winds aloft conditions for each of the flight scenarios in the book. In that connection, the flights are programmed with a wind direction in mind. Thus our takeoff and landing runways will usually agree with an assumed wind as nearly as possible, and where they don't agree, a change in wind direction during the flight, or light and variable winds, are to be understood. As for the Season parameter, why not always Spring? The time for nondaylight flights is predicated upon that season.

Progressive Scenics

The main *Flight Simulator* program is graphically less interesting than are the Scenery Disks, with the exception of the San Francisco Bay area. (The Bay area comes bundled with some versions, and is available as a STAR Scenery Disk for others. It is nearer state-of-the-art.) If you don't own the Scenery Disks we'll fly in this book, you're missing much of the beauty of the simulator; now is the time to make them part of your *Flight Simulator* repertoire. Each successive Scenery Disk represents a quantum upgrade of the simulator itself. *Flight Simulator,* reduced to its essence, is 1) an airplane to fly and 2) geography over which to fly it. And the geography gets more sophisticated with each Scenery Disk.

In the book, as mentioned earlier, we'll fly some scenarios in the main program, especially for pilots new to *Flight Simulator,* so they'll have experienced at least some of the key landmarks in the main-program areas. We'll also fly some situations in the San Francisco Bay area. The major emphasis, however, will be on the later Scenery Disks, primarily because they are graphically more advanced and thus more interesting to fly, and also because they're relatively new to all pilots.

Pausing

You won't always be instructed to pause in this book (and when you are, you'll be told when to unpause—a construction we use without hesitation), but obviously you should occasionally pause and read ahead a bit either to anticipate or catch up with the text, or to better understand a relatively complex set of instructions. If you get completely lost, which is just as possible in the simulator as in the real world (although in this book the chances of it happening are very rare), the best idea is not to start a flight over again. Instead, use your ingenuity and all the resources at hand to find out where you are, and to get back on track to where you want to be. That's the way it is in real-world flying, and it's a more satisfying way to go in *Flight Simulator,* too. Getting lost is good experience (it happens to every pilot), and getting unlost is an equally good experience as well as a great confidence-builder.

Controlling Airspeed

With the proper combination of just two controls, any airplane can be flown at any practical speed—from just above its stalling speed to just below its design maximum or redline. Those two all-important controls are elevator and throttle (the latter controlling rpm). I refer to the elevator control itself, not the elevator trim control.

The basic rules are:

To *increase airspeed,* change to a higher power setting and trim the elevator down.

To *decrease airspeed,* change to a lower power setting and trim the elevator up.

Fine-tune throttle and elevator for straight and level flight at the desired new airspeed.

Once you're flying at a given speed, use power, not elevator, to control your altitude—to climb or descend, or to correct small altitude deviations. This is the technique of choice. Without touching your elevator control, an increase in power setting when you're flying level will cause the airplane to climb, and a decrease will cause it to descend, with little or no change in your airspeed. That's a precise and very satisfying way to fly. (See "Basic Flying Guide," Appendix A, for instructions on making an experimental short flight without using elevator at all.)

Applying the preceding rules, you can actually create a number of different airplanes using just the airframe (or airframes) provided in your simulator version. For example, you can design a fixed-gear, trainer version of the Cessna, as well as a maximum speed, retractable-gear version. Or you can think of your prop or jet aircraft as just one aircraft, but one capable of a wide range of speeds. Thus you can elect to make your takeoff trimmed for slowflight configuration. This will get you airborne faster because, trimmed high, the airplane will fly at a lower airspeed. Then you can stay at that speed, or trim and power for medium or for maximum speed, depending on the distance you're going to fly. For example, here are the Cessna configurations the author currently uses as basics in the 68000 version of the simulator:

I use a reference trim of 121 microadjustable notches (16 quick presses of up elevator starting from full down elevator—abbreviated 16qu). Slowflight (60–65 knots, gear down) is achieved by trimming up 4 × 2qu (four sets of two quick presses of up elevator). I use this higher trim for takeoff, and sometimes leave it on for short or sightseeing flights where speed isn't important. Cruise rpm in this configuration is between 1600 and 1800 (higher altitudes call for higher power settings). For a medium speed (gear still down) of 80–90 knots, I increase power to 1950–2250 rpm, depending on altitude, and trim down to my reference trim (16qu) using 4 × 2qd (four sets of two quick presses of down elevator), in other words, taking off the uptrim that made the aircraft fly slowly, and changing power to suit.

For maximum cruise speed (122–133 knots depending on altitude), I pick up (retract) the gear, trim an additional 4 × 2qd, and reset power to something between 1750–1950 rpm. I say "something between," but I've charted the performance of the Cessna carefully at these trim and power settings, so I know for example (simply by checking my homemade chart) that about 1900 rpm is needed in maximum cruise configuration to fly straight and level at 3500 feet. At 5000 feet I need 1950 rpm, and at 500 feet the initial power setting should be 1750. I also know that my climbout power setting after takeoff should be 2050 rpm if I'll stay in slowflight, 2300 if I'll trim down for medium-speed configuration (beginning as soon as I'm airborne), and 1950 or 2000 rpm if I'll retract the gear and trim down another 4 × 2qd, for a total of 8 × 2qd, for maximum cruise configuration.

In flight, I can change speeds readily using the same trims and power changes—and where applicable, gear positions—to suit myself and/or the situation. The three speed ranges give me all the flexibility I need. I have similar trim and power techniques for flying the Learjet, beginning with a trim of 8 × 2qu (from the same 16qu reference trim) for a fixed-gear, trainer-type jet that flies at an average 115 knots to a full-performance version that pushes 400 knots.

Note that the use of sets of two quick presses is not arbitrary. I deliberately work with the two-quick-presses value because it provides smooth and efficient inflight trimming, and is also easy to remember. Trimming by slow presses of the elevator keys takes too long, and more than two quick presses results in drastic pitch attitudes. By standardizing on groups of four sets of two quick presses each, trimming for a new speed becomes a relatively simple matter. And I just accept the speed range that results from application of the easy formula. You needn't use four sets—how many sets depends on your specific aircraft—but using n sets of 2q up or down will get the job done efficiently and smoothly.

I urge you to follow some such technique to create your own speeds, and a performance chart that tells you where to set your power (for each of three speed trims) for altitudes of, say, 1000 to 5000 feet in steps of 500 feet to altitude 2500, and then steps of 1000 feet to an altitude of 5000 feet. It's worth the work involved, and will add immeasurably to your flight professionalism, precision, and overall skills—not to mention your satisfaction.

As an example, below is my chart for the Cessna (Amiga and Atari ST versions). Note that my designations C42E, C16E, C42R (that I can use in situation titles) describe both the trim and the gear position, the reference or *center* trim being 16qu from full down, the E meaning gear is extended, and the R, retracted. 42E is an abbreviation for 4 × 2qu from reference trim, gear down, and 42R is an abbreviation for 4 × 2qd from reference trim, gear retracted. The chart is arranged in order of increasing speeds, which are approximately (at 5000 feet), 65, 95, and 133 knots (lower at lower altitudes). The digit after the decimal point is my way of describing where in the four-notch range of one rpm reading (.0 to .3) the optimum setting is. Frequently a flight will call for a one- or two-notch increase or decrease of the throttle settings shown, but they are good values with which to start.

Cessna Performance Chart (Amiga/Atari ST)

A/C	Climb RPM	Cruise 1000'	RPMs 1500'	2000'	2500'	3500'	4500'	5000'	Descent RPM
C42E	2050.3	1650.0	1650.0	1650.1	1650.3	1700.3	1750.3	1800.1	1100.3
C16E*	2300.0	2000.0	2050.0	2050.0	2100.0	2150.1	2200.2	2250.1	1700.3
C42R	1950.3	1800.0	1800.0	1800.1	1850.0	1900.0	1950.0	1950.0	1600.2

* 68000 en route mode, described in first flight. Aircraft is trimmed 3qu +3sd from SLEW default for 82 KIAS (approximate) at 1500'. The result is the same as trimming 16qu from full down elevator.

About the Mouse, Joystick, and Rudder

I'll not belabor this point (and I know old habits are hard to change), but in my books I have consistently recommended using the keypad or keyboard yoke (in preference to the mouse or joystick), if such is provided by your version. The keyboard yoke affords a precision that simply isn't possible with either of the latter, and more closely simulates proportional control. Further, I recommend disabling autocoordination of the rudder and aileron. Independent control of your rudder (and on the ground, nosewheel) makes turning to and holding headings easier, and is a great boon on landing approaches. So in this book when I refer to *yawing* the nose around a few degrees to a given heading, I'm referring to using your rudder. If you elect to keep autocoordination, then simply substitute an aileron turn.

View Standardization

For versions of *Flight Simulator* that provide Tower and Spot Plane views, positioning in this book is optimized for the following settings:

Main 3D Spot Plane. View from rear, fast transition, distance 150 feet, altitude 20 feet, preference Roll. (These settings are helpful for taxiing the aircraft, and checking gear position in flight.)

2nd 3D Spot Plane. View from right side, fast transition, distance 150 feet, altitude 0 feet, preference Roll. (These settings, in particular the zero altitude, are useful for observing aircraft pitch attitude in flight, for example, straight and level, climb, descend. In instant-replayed landing approaches, the distance and altitude parameters and the side view help in evaluating flare and touchdown performance. For instance: "Did I touch down on the main gear, or smack down nosewheel first?")

Spot Plane view ZOOM factors depend on the size of the display screen (the degree of reduction, if any, of the instrument panel). For the NAV-capable panel described in "Opening Up," below, the author standardizes on a zoom factor of 0.71 for the out-the-windshield views and for both spot plane views.

The majority of Tower views suggested for the various scenarios are not Tower views per se, but rather the views of a ground observer who is usually positioned close to the runway and at a realistically human height. Note in the very first scenario that the tower altitude is a couple of feet lower than the airport elevation, yet the observer is not underground; instead, the view is at a natural eye-level, and simulates what you would see if you stood back from your plane to look it over. (The Tower altitude in the first scenario establishes the *Odyssey* standard, and will usually carry over successfully to the next and the next scenario, obviating the need to type in the new altitude. This is not always the case, however.) Initial ZOOM factor for the tower view is 1.00 in all cases, but ZOOM should be used freely at all times to obtain the optimum tower view. (For the purposes of this book, ZOOMing other views is not recommended, particularly if you've adjusted your aspect ratio to suit a custom panel configuration as described below.)

Opening Up

One final word before we begin our *Odyssey.* If you have a version of *Flight Simulator* that permits you to enlarge the main display by abbreviating the instrument panel, I urge you to do so. I fly virtually all the time with the instrument panel reduced in one of two ways:

For contact flying (navigating solely by visual reference) I shrink the panel so the clock compartment is aligned with the bottom of the screen (I call this the Time or T panel), after setting the ZOOM to .65 for the Main, Main Spot, and second 3D Spot views.

For flights that involve VOR navigation, I shrink the panel so the NAV 1 radio compartment is aligned with the bottom of the screen. I can still tune the NAV, and can see the DME readout. I don't need NAV 2 or its associated OBS, or the turn coordinator, VSI, or other instruments. I know from my performance chart what power settings will result in a standard (500 FPM, (Feet Per Minute)) climb or descent. I can use both the visual and artificial horizons for determining my degree of bank. The altimeter gives me a sensitive indication of whether I'm flying level or losing or gaining altitude; a notch of power either way will correct such situations. The artificial horizon is my bank indicator, and advises me as to pitch attitude when I have no outside horizon. My reward for dispensing with some of the instruments is a greatly enhanced view of the world out the windows. To compensate for the different aspect ratio of the main and spot-plane views, I set zoom for this NAV or N version of the panel to 0.71 and leave it there (this and the time-panel setting correspond nicely to a zoom factor of 1.00 with the normal display).

And now—Bon Voyage!

En Route Starter
Chart: Chicago Area
Title: See text
Ground Coordinates:
   Aircraft: N16581 (16582.074), E16507 (16506.994)
   Tower: N16581.994, E16507.046
Altitude:
   Aircraft: 0 (simulator will set to approx. 785)
   Tower: 782 (recheck after entering all parameters)
Heading: 180
Time: Daylight (07:01)
General: Note that Titles will be suggested for those who have situation titling capability. If a flight begins on the ground, we use the expression "Ground Coordinates," if it begins in the air, it's "En Route Coordinates." Aircraft altitude should always be set to 0 for flights beginning on the ground; the simulator will find the appropriate altitude. Tower altitude is often misconstrued by the simulator, and so, should be rechecked if you plan to take tower views.

You're in position for takeoff at Paxton Airport, Paxton, Illinois, on Runway 18. You'll find Paxton, the county seat of Ford County, on the lower third of your Chicago Area chart.

Before creating our generic en route situation, you may want to set up and save one or more on-the-ground configurations, and now's the time to do it. For example, if you're flying an earlier version, you may want to disable autocoordination and set up your favorite takeoff configuration. If flying the 68000 version, you may want to do the same and also create the NAV and Time panels described earlier (suggested titles GROUND/N PANEL and, if you also wish to set up the T panel, GROUND/T PANEL); you could also set up other configurations of your choosing. (If NAV 1 is needed in a flight, it will be shown as a "Special Requirement" at the outset of a chapter.) For flights that begin on the ground, you can then recall your ready aircraft, enter the coordinates given at the beginning of each chapter, set up the specific compass heading, and be all ready to go.

If you have your ground starter saved now, you're ready to create and save your en route starter. Here's how:

Amiga and Atari ST Pilots Only. Regardless of the trim you may use for your usual or favorite takeoff (that should already be saved as described earlier), you'll use a special trim now that will make it easy to get to and save the optimum en route configuration. Pause and enable SLEW. This sets your elevator to the *default* trim. Next, disable SLEW. Then apply 3qu (three quick presses of the up elevator key), followed by 3sd (three slow presses of down elevator, pausing slightly between each). This trim-restoring procedure—3qu + 3sd—is the procedure you'll always use for en route situations after SLEWing to the prescribed compass heading. Now, when you're ready, put on full power for the takeoff roll. Use no elevator. The airplane will autorotate at 80-85 KIAS and fly itself off. Leave your gear down. When you're airborne, reduce power to 2300 rpm for your climbout (note that your VSI (Vertical Speed Indicator) will show a climb of about 500 FPM). Climb until you reach about 1500 feet (the specific altitude isn't critical), then reduce throttle for an rpm reading of 2050.0 (lowest notch that still reads 2050). Your plane will settle into straight and level flight at 80-85 KIAS. When everything is stabilized, pause and skip to the "En Route Save" section of this text below.

Macintosh Pilots Only. Take off in your normal manner, but don't retract your gear. Climb to about 1500 feet and level off. If your airspeed is 80–90 knots, go to the "En Route Save" section of this text below. If not, follow the rules under Controlling Airspeed above to adjust elevator and power until you are straight and level at an airspeed of 80–90 KIAS. Take all the time you need to get this thing right. You'll be using the mode all through this book. When you're satisfied that you're straight and level, at the described airspeed, and at or near an altitude of 1500 feet (you can change altitude using the NAV menu and POSITION SET), pause and save the situation as TEMPORARY. Then observe your elevator position indicator carefully, and make a note of where it is in relation to the indices of the gauge. Next, watching the indicator and noting where it moves to, temporarily enable SLEW. This automatically resets the default trim. Next, restore your earlier trim, this time making a note of how many notches of movement separate the default trim and the medium-speed trim at which you arrived. Do this several times until you're convinced you have it mastered. Then, each time we use an en route situation in this book, you'll follow this "restoration" procedure after SLEWing. (Also, you now know precisely how to fly your Cessna at medium airspeed, so it was worth the trouble.) Next, recall TEMPORARY and delete it, and go to the "En Route Save" section below.

Earlier Version Pilots Only. (IBM PC and compatibles, PCjr, Commodore 64, Apple II series, Atari 800/XL/XE) You don't even need to take off—simply pause, go into the Editor, and set the following parameters (leave North and East where they are):

Altitude: 1500
Pitch: If flying Cessna, 0; if flying Piper, 359
Bank: 0
Airspeed: If Cessna, 80; if Piper, 84
Throttle: If Cessna, 12287; if Piper, 6144
Rudder and Ailerons: 32767
Flaps: 0
Elevators: If Cessna, 39679; if Piper, 40959

Exit the Editor, unpause, and fly a few seconds until the aircraft is stabilized (if needed, make minor adjustments in throttle or trim as described under Controlling Airspeed above) and then continue with the "En Route Save" section below.

En Route Save

Whatever version you're flying, you should now be straight and level at 80–90 knots at about 1500 feet, and with the simulation paused. Save the situation, titling it (or if your version doesn't accommodate titling, referencing it) as ENROUTE/ GENERIC, or if you can adjust your instrument panel and wish to fly with both Time and NAV panels, set up those panels and use the titles ENROUTE/N PANEL and EN-ROUTE/T PANEL. (If you want to use just one abbreviated panel, let it be the NAV panel, since we'll have to tune NAV 1 on a number of flights. Note that ZOOM can be set independently for the MAIN 3D view, MAIN 3D Spot Plane View, and second 3D Spot Plane view. I set them all to .65 for the T panel and .71 for the N panel, as described earlier.)

Now we're finished with preliminaries. Let our Odyssey begin.

CHAPTER TWO
Main Program
Highlights

Statue of Liberty

Chart: New York
Title: STATUE LIBERTY
En Route Coordinates:
  Aircraft: N17048, E20974
  Tower: ——
Altitude:
  Aircraft: 147
  Tower: ——
Heading: 317
Time: Daylight

What better introduction to the New York area than the lady herself? Standing in New York Harbor on Liberty Island, she's a regal 151 feet high including her torch. (But alas!—in real life the torch is in her right hand.)

The Statue of Liberty was designed by Gustave Eiffel, who also created the Eiffel Tower (which we'll see later in our travels). She was a gift to the U.S. from the people of France, commemorating the first centennial of United States independence. The book in her hand is inscribed "July 4, 1776." Can you believe the U.S. Congress instituted a national lottery in that very same year so long ago? What goes around comes around.

Take left-side views as you fly by.

World Trade Center Towers

Chart: New York
Title: TRADE CNTR TWRS
En Route Coordinates:
   Aircraft: N17056, E20980
   Tower: ——
Altitude:
   Aircraft: 647
   Tower: ——
Heading: 50
Time: Daylight

    I know it looks a little hairy, but I'm almost certain you can fly through there without a scratch.

    New York City thought the World Trade Center Towers, dedicated in 1973, would be the world's tallest buildings (at 1353 feet) for a long time to come. But the Sears Tower in Chicago, completed the same year, was deliberately designed to top them by about 100 feet, and is the world's tallest (we'll have a look at it soon).

    When (or if) you get safely through, the 1250-foot Empire State Building will be just ahead of you. This landmark was the world's tallest building until the other three came along. Structured of steel, it nevertheless swayed nearly three inches in a 100-mph gale in 1936.

New York's Finest

Chart: New York
Title: INBOUND LGA 22
En Route Coordinates:
   Aircraft: N17122, E21047
   Tower: N17095.510, E21027.074
Altitude:
   Aircraft: 1500
   Tower: 28
Heading: 254
Time: Daylight

You're over the southern tip of Long Island Sound, on a diagonal approach to and cleared to land on Runway 22 at La Guardia Airport. The near bridge is the Throg's Neck and the other one is the Bronx-Whitestone. You see a little of the Bronx on your right. La Guardia is on the Queens side of the East River, the latter being the name of the continuation of Long Island Sound at this point. Runway 22 reaches right out to the water's edge. Field elevation is 22 feet.

You'll want to start your descent promptly. Wait to turn to your final approach until the runway is well to the left on your windshield, and appears almost straight. When you're lined up, try controlling and observing your flare (if you have tower-view capability), as seen by the ground observer.

La Guardia, for simulator pilots, is the best of the two airports close to Manhattan. Its runways are paved, whereas the runways at JFK are just confusing outlines on the grass. (The highly undesirable outline-airport syndrome slowly fades away, happily, with the advent of the Scenery Disks.)

What's Left?

Chart: New York
Title: LONG FNL JFK 4L
En Route Coordinates:
  Aircraft: N16972, E21047
  Tower: N17019.604, E21065.787
Altitude:
  Aircraft: 1500
  Tower: 14
Heading: 044
Time: Daylight

This approach will show you what I mean about outline-only airports. You're more or less lined up on a long final for Runway 4 Left at John F. Kennedy International. But even when the airport "blossoms," how are you to determine runways from taxiways? Is 4L the runway with the centerline, in which case 4R is the strip at the extreme right? Or is the centerlined runway 4R, while 4L is the outlined area that looks like it might be a runway on the other side of what looks like a divider?

Actually 4L is the runway with the centerline, but if you've never landed on it before, you'd have to be a seer to know. And if you had approached JFK from some random direction, rather than on a relative straight-in heading, you'd have to be omniscient to pick out any runway before you were virtually at the center of things.

Field elevation is 12 feet.

Manhattan Bridge Caper 1

Chart: New York
Title: MNHTTN BRIDGE 1
En Route Coordinates:
  Aircraft: N17056, E20996
  Tower: ——
Altitude:
  Aircraft: 75
  Tower: ——
Heading: 278
Time: Daylight

The idea here is to fly between the roadway and the sus-pension girders, not over them. You'll have to immediately back off on your power and get down a bit lower. Don't get too low, however—you'll be in the East River or fly smack into the cars tooling across Manhattan Bridge. Once safely past the bridge, put on some power again in a hurry, or you'll still wind up wet. Your pass-through point is just to the right of the center of the structure.

This magnificent bridge, completed in 1909, has a main suspension span of 1470 feet, and carries eight railroad tracks and two footpaths in addition to its roadway.

Manhattan Bridge Caper 2

Chart: New York
Title: MNHTTN BRIDGE 2
En Route Coordinates:
  Aircraft: N17045, E20995
  Tower: ——
Altitude:
  Aircraft: 650
  Tower: ——
Heading: 028
Time: Daylight

You're flying over Flatbush, Brooklyn. You are a movie
stunt pilot, and your assignment here is to land on Manhattan
Bridge. The scene calls for you to touch down as close to the
near edge of the bridge roadway as possible. As you can see,
you have your work cut out for you. Thoughtfully, director
Steven Spielhof made arrangements for you to be paid in advance. Hopefully, you've made all the other necessary arrangements.

Roots

Chart: Chicago
Title: LONG FNL CGX 18
En Route Coordinates:
   Aircraft: N17215, E16670
   Tower: N17188.339, E16670.893
Altitude:
   Aircraft: 1500
   Tower: See text
Heading: 180
Time: Dawn (06:01)

We can't be in the main program and not pay homage to Merrill C. Meigs airport. It's the "home" airport of the earlier versions of *Flight Simulator*—perhaps it's the home of the version you're flying now—and where many a simulator pilot took an all-too-popular "crash" course. The CGX in the title is the official airport code for Meigs (we'll use such codes in titles wherever appropriate, since they are standard abbreviations).

Just before touchdown

If (in tower-capable versions) the tower view looks right, leave the altitude alone, whatever it is. If it doesn't—for instance the observer appears to be a mole in its burrow—try ALT 595. The simulator can get very confused at Meigs. When the tower view is right, however, it's a beauty in this scenario.

Altitude is often misconstrued by the simulator, so check it and if necessary reset it to 1500 feet. (On some occasions, in some versions, the simulator will incorrectly interpret all inflight altitudes and ground elevations in the same area. In those cases, the only remedy I know of is to recall a situation that has the aircraft on the ground, and then proceed to recall the desired inflight mode. This is the procedure to use if what you see on the screen, together with a queer altimeter reading, is not what you expected.)

You're on an early morning approach to Runway 18 at Meigs, one of the prettier dawn/dusk approaches in the Chicago area. The buildings you can see are the John Hancock Building and, out the right side, Sears Tower.

Chicago was the first city in the U.S. to have skyscrapers, and the Sears Tower is the world's tallest. When you sit in the Skydeck there, you're at an altitude of 1353 feet—not much below your present inflight altitude. The 94-floor Hancock building (no midget, either) is unusual in that it comprises both commercial and residential space, with the result that some residents commute to work by elevator (great when it's snowing outside).

Due to the early hour, you can't tell what's water and what's land below you, but Meigs is virtually surrounded by the waters of Lake Michigan and Burnham Park Harbor. Only a thin peninsula just this side of the runway keeps it from being an island. On the tip of the peninsula is the Adler Planetarium, directly opposite the Field Museum of Natural History in Chicago proper. The colorful lakefront marinas and Grant Park are strung along Chicago Harbor, this side of Meigs.

Start letting down for your landing when the Hancock building is off your right wingtip. You're seeing the outline of the entire airport complex at this distance, and the lie of the runway is not readily apparent, so don't be in a hurry to yaw left or right.

When the runway itself takes shape, do what you feel

you should if you need to improve your alignment. And keep on doing that, right down to the threshold. Use power changes to improve your final approach. If you feel you're high, reduce power, or put on some flaps to permit a steeper descent; if low, increase power or apply some up elevator to stretch the final approach. Try to keep the runway threshold at or slightly below the center of your windshield, all the way down.

Elevation at Meigs is just under 600 feet.

For a whole different perspective, you can advance the time one hour and fly the preceding situation in daylight.

Stupendous Colossal

Chart: New York
Title: FNL BRDGEPRT 06
En Route Coordinates:
  Aircraft: N17258, E21228
  Tower: N17283.678, E21248.226
Altitude:
  Aircraft: 1500
  Tower: 14
Heading: 061
Time: Daylight

You're on final approach to Runway 06 at Igor I. Sikorski Memorial Airport in Bridgeport, CT. This town had no less a character for mayor in bygone days than Phineas T. Barnum, the circus entrepreneur. Born in 1810, he began his show business career at the age of 25 by exhibiting a black woman, Joyce Heth, whom he claimed was over 160 years old and had been George Washington's nurse. In 1841 he opened the so-called "American Museum," which was an exhibition of freaks and curiosities, including the dwarf Tom Thumb and The Bearded Lady. In 1850 he made a genuine contribution to culture by managing an American tour for coloratura soprano Jenny Lind, the *Swedish Nightingale,* and one of the most famous opera stars and recitalists of her time. The first performance of Barnum's circus, "The Greatest Show on Earth," was in Brooklyn in 1871, and ten years later he merged with rival showman James Bailey to form the famous Barnum and Bailey Circus.

Your approach is over Long Island Sound, and airport elevation is 17 feet. (The tower position is a short way up the runway, and is a beauty for watching yourself come in, or replaying your approach.)

A Fair Approach

Chart: Seattle
Title: A FAIR APPROACH
En Route Coordinates:
  Aircraft: N21426, E6589
  Tower: N21372.019, E6595.9321
Altitude:
  Aircraft: 1500
  Tower: 15
Heading: 129
Time: Dusk (19:01)

Read before you unpause:
The Seattle area is easily the most beautiful of the four original simulator areas. I suspect it was the last to be digitized, because its areas of light and dark landscape and the extraordinary detailing of Puget Sound and Lake Washington are without rival until we get to the San Francisco Bay area and the scenery disks. Out your left windows you'll see some of the Cascade Range. It's those mountains that confine the mostly-winter rains to the Puget Sound area, making it so green and so island-laced. It's easy to understand why one in every four families in Seattle owns a boat.

Ice-capped Mount Rainier is on the horizon. A sleeping volcano, it rises 14,410 feet into—and is often shrouded in—the clouds. The nation's first Mt. Everest team trained on its glacial heights. Campers and backpackers are seen on the 90-mile Wonderland Trail that encircles Mount Rainier National Park, at the foot of the mountain. (Were you to fly to the other side of the simulated mountain, you'd discover a curious fact or two. Try it sometime.)

Now unpause and watch that vertical something on the shore of Puget Sound. For about ten seconds, nothing will happen. But when you've about decided it's simply a vertical line, it will blossom into three dimensions, and you'll be viewing the Space Needle at Seattle Center. Symbol of the 1962 World's Fair here, it's an observation tower crowned with a revolving restaurant—an idea that has spawned many imitations ever since. Watch it pass by out the left side.

After you've passed the Space Needle, continue toward what looks like an airport shaping up on this side of Interstate

5. It's Boeing Field, also known as King County International, and you're on a long final to its Runway 13. Actually the field has parallel strips, but you're interested in 13 Left, the one that will eventually turn out to have a centerline (neither one, in the simulation, is paved; both are simply outlines on the grass). This is one of the most confusing airports to approach in the simulator world (and that's saying something). You'll see what I mean when you're closer in. The whole area suddenly opens up like a late-blooming flower, giving no clue as to where the runways are. But persevere in your heading until you see a real centerline. That's your runway.

Airport elevation is 437 feet.

A word about simulated airports that are, like this one in Seattle, just outlines on the grass . . . and also about some other problems in *Flight Simulator.*

It's no wonder simulator pilots complain about the difficulties of making decent landings. If all airports were like this one in Seattle, we could chalk it up to some difficulty or problem in digitizing solid runways. But for some strange reason, while many of the largest airports are, incomprehensibly, fields of grass, most little airports (and some big ones), are beautifully paved and marked off, and thus readily discernible from the air. In New York, big La Guardia is paved, and its runways are visible from miles out, while big JFK is just a confusing scrawl of lines at any and all distances. In the Amiga version, at least, the whole Boston area, including Logan International, is a pale blue monstrosity (not paved, not grass, but a sickly blue for miles) as if someone spilled a pail of paint over it—an impossible place to think of flying to or from once you've seen it. In Chicago, the big airports— Midway and O'Hare—are like JFK. Why isn't it possible to pave the runways, and let the taxiways and other area outlines simply be outlines? It's the runways we need to see from the air, and yet there are some airports (we'll visit some in this book) that are models of definition, where both runways and taxiways—and ramps too—are paved. They're easy to taxi around on, realistic, and readily picked out from the air. It can be done, so why not do it?

I admire the amazing achievements of *Flight Simulator* more than anything else in the microcomputer world. But that doesn't keep me from wondering about some of the notorious lapses of judgment and irritating bugs that beset it, and us who love to fly it. Here's just a cursory sampling, Amiga version, and in parentheses some possible though perhaps too pat suggestions for correcting them:

⊙ Mountains are the same color as the surrounding landscape, so you can't really sense them as mountains. (Make mountains a different color than that of the surrounding landscape. It's been done in some places. Why not every place?)

⊙ Mountains are totally invisible at night. (Make mountains at night a dark gray or something so they can be distinguished.)

⊙ Mountains of other-worldly colors, even in computers that support thousands of colors, are destroying all illusion of reality. (Color the mountains in earthtones, or at least in shades of green distinguishable from the landscape greens.)

⊙ Oceans, lakes and reservoirs are totally inseparable from land masses at dawn, dusk or night. (Make bodies of water a shade of dark blue or gray, so they can be distinguished from land masses in dawn/dusk/night flights.)

⊙ Highways are almost always a glaring, brittle white—night and day. (Make highways a less intense color; gray them down.)

⊙ The aircraft's wings are the same glaring white as highways, night or day. It seems unrealistic to look out at blackness past that hospital-white wing. (Gray the wing down for dawn, dusk, and night.)

⊙ The instrument panel is too bright at night, unrealistic by contrast with the world outside. (Gray the instruments down at night, and make the panel background dark blue or black—darken the whole thing to give a feeling of night. Or leave the instruments as they are, so they'll look lighted, but make the panel background dark blue or black.)

⊙ The night skies are too intensely black. No sky, moon or not, was ever so black as the simulator sky at night. Night feels better as a deep, rich, dark blue. (Make night a deep, rich, dark blue. Make it more like dawn or dusk, or let dawn/dusk be the night simulation and lighten up dawn and dusk, which are too dark anyway. As a bare minimum, make the dawn/dusk sky a shade of gray rather than blue.)

⊙ The cityscape buildings are too intensely white (or some-

27

times black). (Gray the white ones down; lighten the intensely black ones.)

⊙ There is water/land confusion at numerous waterside airport locations. The sky flashes with the color of nearby water, or a water diagonal superimposes itself on the sky. This problem is rife in the Amiga version. (Unconfuse the water/land programming near large bodies of water.) There is also land/land confusion. Right here, stopped and with my engine at idle on Boeing Field, my sky is split by a right triangle of dark green, the color of Mount Rainier. I turn the aircraft left a few degrees and the phenomenon disappears.

⊙ DME (Distance Measuring Equipment) reading is sometimes nautical miles, sometimes statute miles; there is no way for the pilot to discern the two. (Program the DME reading with one or the other, advise which, and be consistent.)

⊙ There are abrupt altitude changes of hundreds of feet en route, frequently after disk accesses. (Let the programmers all work with the same altitude references?)

⊙ Hidden surface removals (68000 series) hide or remove the wrong surfaces—a bug that results (for instance) in mountains being superimposed on foregrounds instead of the other way around. (Lay down the landscape first, in order of farthest to nearest; then lay down the features man puts on the landscape.

I'll stop (for now) at the magic number of 13. But I must add that, despite all these complaints, if I were somehow deprived of *Flight Simulator* I really don't know how I'd face the world.

Narrows Escape

Chart: Seattle
Title: NARROWS ESCAPE
En Route Coordinates:
 Aircraft: N21270, E6460
 Tower: N21295.592, 6477.0819
Altitude:
 Aircraft: 1228
 Tower: 25
Heading: 352
Time: Daylight

You're on final approach to Runway 35, Tacoma Narrows Airport, Tacoma, Washington. That big body of water you see is Commencement Bay, one of the southern bays of Puget Sound. The Tacoma Narrows runway is unusual in that it reaches right out into the bay, so you'd best make your approach an accurate one. On the way down, consider that in Tacoma stands the world's tallest totem pole, carved by Indians from a single giant tree.

Try not to be low man on it.

Airport elevation is about 300 feet.

A Gander at Hughes

Chart: Los Angeles
Title: GANDER @ HUGHES
En Route Coordinates:
  Aircraft: N15370, E5756
  Tower: N15386.327, E5810.2457
Altitude:
  Aircraft: 1230
  Tower: 26
Heading: 042
Time: Daylight

If the Seattle area marks the scenic pinnacle of the original four simulator areas, then the Los Angeles area does the same for the scenic pits. We'll make just one stop here, and then be off to greener pastures in the San Francisco Bay area (*greener* is hardly the word, seeing that in the main program we know the color green all too well).

You're inbound for a private airport, Hughes, lodged between Marina del Rey, visible just left of your course, and the parallel runways of Los Angeles International. Proceed with your approach for a landing on Runway 04.

Marina del Rey, just south of Venice, California in Santa Monica Bay, was created by man, not nature, and provides docking facilities for an incredible 6,000 small boats. You'll get a better idea of its shape as you get closer. Replete with boutiques and restaurants as well as sports and fishing craft, the marina's Fisherman's Village is patterned after New England prototypes.

The airport to the left of Marina del Rey is Santa Monica Municipal.

The airport you're headed for is a very confusing one to get around on, considering it has just one strip, but this scenario will plunk you down on that strip without problems.

Howard Hughes, for whose Hughes Aircraft Company this airport is named, is probably best known for his reputation as one of the richest, most eccentric, and most reclusive men in America, as well as for his mammoth seaplane The Spruce Goose, (which made one brief low-level flight—and headlines—with Hughes at the controls, when he was supposed to simply taxi it over the water for testing purposes).

Old-timers will remember his motion picture, *Hell's Angels.* And he did make a couple of important contributions to aviation. In 1935 he set a world speed record of 352 miles per hour in a plane of his own design. Two years later he crossed the continent eastward in the record time of 7 hours, 28 minutes. And in July of 1938, he and four companions completed a record flight around the world in 3 days, 19 hours, and 8 minutes. Years of lawsuits over his will followed his death in 1976, and we may not have heard the last of the litigants yet.

Elevation at Hughes is 136 feet. The runway has no centerline, and there's an outlined turnaround area at its near end. In the distance are the San Gabriel and San Bernardino mountains.

CHAPTER THREE
San Francisco Bay Area

Something Fishy

Chart: San Francisco
Title: SOMETHING FISHY
Ground Coordinates:
  Aircraft: N17422 (17422.296), E5074 (5073.8229)
  Tower: N17420.826, E5074.4836
Altitude:
  Aircraft: 0
  Tower: 28
Heading: 122
Time: Daylight

    As I mentioned earlier, I've covered the San Francisco Bay area quite thoroughly in earlier books, specifically *Runway USA* and *Flying Flight Simulator;* the latter for the Amiga, Atari ST, and Macintosh computers. Further, the San Francisco STAR Scenery Disk (for the earlier versions) and the San Francisco and Bay areas as bundled with the later versions, vary somewhat, particularly regarding bugs. And those bugs (the ones I'm speaking of are found mostly in San Francisco) are associated, in particular, with mountains. So it's not feasible to cover San Francisco extensively in a book that's not machine- and version-specific. There is also a third rendering of the San Francisco area. It's in Scenery Disk 3, one of a now sorely outdated and I would think ill-fated Western Set of six Scenery Disks released for the earlier versions of *Flight Simulator.* While these disks cover some fascinating areas of the U.S., and I devoted a whole book (*Runway USA*) to them, they were premature insofar as detail was concerned. Fast on their heels, the STAR version of San Francisco, along with the Japan Scenery Disk, opened up new vistas in flight simulation. The Western Set, unfortunately, trailed far behind these two in scenic interest and detail, and still further behind the more recent Scenery Disks 7, 11 and Western Europe. (It's my understanding that the Western Set will be updated and newly released in the not-too-distant future—an event to which we all, I'm sure, look forward eagerly.)

That said, we'll concentrate on having a bit of fun in the immediate area of San Francisco Bay and the Golden Gate.

The Golden Gate is, of course, not a bridge but the body of water that flows between San Francisco and the Marin Peninsula, connecting San Francisco Bay and the Pacific Ocean. The Golden Gate Bridge, named for the body of water, connects the city of San Francisco with Sausalito, on the other side of the Golden Gate, and other neighboring cities to the north.

This first scenario puts you on an "improvised" takeoff and landing strip right on the waterfront. In fact, you're on a dock at Fishermen's Wharf, pointed toward the San Francisco-Oakland Bay Bridge and some downtown buildings. The Golden Gate Bridge is behind you to the right.

Obviously, your best short-field takeoff technique is called for here. The parenthetical North and East parameters give later-version pilots all of the wharf; but for those of you without fractional parameter capability, this will be a short takeoff indeed. However, if you use a little of the grass as well as all of the wharf, you'll get airborne okay.

Proceed with your takeoff. (If you have Tower capability, watch from that vantage point, and be prepared to duck.) Throttle back quickly for a 500-FPM climb (to keep your altitude low), skim the buildings on your right, and then turn left to head over the nearest of the Bay Bridge's four arches. Pour on some power if you need it to clear the girders.

The airport on the other side of the bay is Nimitz Field.

And surprise!—you'll shoot a landing on Runway 07 over there— elevation 17 feet—so work to get into position.

(After these shenanigans, if everyone in the Bay area doesn't know about you already, they will after the 6 o'clock news.)

Fisherman's Luck

Chart: San Francisco
Title: FISHERMANS LUCK
En Route Coordinates:
  Aircraft: N17428, E5071
  Tower: N17420.826, E5074.3861
Altitude:
  Aircraft: 560
  Tower: 28
Heading: 121
Time: Daylight

Recognize that wharf straight ahead? It should be a cinch to set the airplane down on it, so go ahead and do it. But don't use any of the grass beyond the wharf. And, of course, don't use any of the water, on any side. What you can use, naturally, is your flaps and, at the last, your brakes. Remember that flaps let you descend more steeply, without undue increase in airspeed, and significantly lower the stalling speed of the aircraft.

San Francisco Wharfs

If you use flaps, remember to dump them (zero them) after you've landed, or they'll carry right over to the next scenario you save.

Wharf Turnabout

Chart: San Francisco
Title: WHARF TURNABOUT
En Route Coordinates:
  Aircraft: N17411, E5079
  Tower: Same as prior scenario
Altitude:
  Aircraft: 1224
  Tower: Same as prior scenario
Heading: 298
Time: Daylight

Aw, come on! It's the same wharf. You're just landing from the opposite direction. Same as over the Bay, only this time it's over the land.
(Just as a little reminder, remember what flaps do, as mentioned in the prior scenario. This is one occasion where they'll come in very handy indeed.)

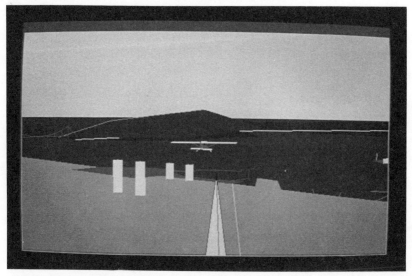

Over the tip of Transamerica

Wave at the folks in the office building windows as you make your descent. It'll reassure them.

(If you touch down on the grass instead of the wharf, you lose.)

Swingin' On the Gate

Chart: San Francisco
Title: SWINGIN ON GATE
En Route Coordinates:
  Aircraft: N17430, E5069
  Tower: N17434.694, E5055.4641
Altitude:
  Aircraft: 743
  Tower: 15
Heading: 254
Time: Daylight

That strip of grass beyond the bridge, between the water and the foot of the mountain, looks like an ideal landing strip. And it is. Judge your approach carefully, and you can pass over the end of the bridge at low, low altitude—maybe even startle a few motorists down there in the traffic.

Once you're on the ground, maybe you'll want to get into position for takeoff in the opposite direction, and save this as a special flying field in the Bay area. It's a neat place to fly from and to.

Elevation is 17 feet.

San Francisco was under the control of the Spanish, who called it Yerba Buena, until 1846, when it was taken by the United States. Two years later it was hustled into growth by the California Gold Rush, and later by the advent of the transcontinental railroad. The famous earthquake and fire occurred in April, 1906. During World War II the city was an embarkation point for campaigns in the Pacific, and was the scene of the drafting of the United Nations Charter and the signing of the Japanese Peace Treaty.

Doll of a Valley

Chart: San Francisco
Title: LAKE DEL VALLE
Ground Coordinates:
 Aircraft: N17245 (17245.148), E5272 (5271.8619)
 Tower: N17245.253, E5271.9477
Altitude:
 Aircraft: 0
 Tower: 14
Heading: 137
Time: Daylight

This beautiful setting for a personal flying field is alongside the water in California's Lake Del Valle State Recreation Area, about 37 miles from San Francisco.

When you feel like flying for the sheer pleasure of it, mountainous areas are a good choice. They provide challenge when you want it, scenic vistas to enjoy, and lazy trails to wind in and out of when you just want to tool around.

There aren't that many really ideal mountainous areas in the simulator, and too many of those are beset with bugs in at least some versions. Here you have Lake Del Valle for contrast, four mountains in the immediate area, and two more behind you. The lake is nestled in a valley. One of the best airports in the Bay area—Livermore Municipal—is within easy reach.

Before you fly, study the location on your map. You're in position for takeoff. The smaller body of water to the west is San Antonio Reservoir. When you zoom out, you can see two highways, I-205 and I-580, merging. They continue as one highway, I-580, leading to Livermore. Zoom in and note that your landing area is along the knife-like edge of the southeastern tip of the lake. You can land here, of course, from either direction.

Now go ahead and take off, and let's look around a bit.

Fly straight up the valley while you climb to 1000 feet. (I regret very much that, in the Amiga version, there is another of those sky bugs—even in this beautiful place. The ground regularly flickers and disappears, and sky intermittently takes its place, disembodying the mountains. This altogether unwelcome phenomenon can be defeated by taking a Spot Plane view, or views out the side, but that destroys the mood. The bug seems to wear itself out after some minutes of flight, only to return again as you maneuver.)

When you can see out the left side that you'll clear the mountain if you make a left turn, make one, taking up a heading of about 050 degrees. Hold that heading until you're beyond the end of the mountain, then turn left again to a heading of about 320, or whatever points you up this second valley (thankfully the Amiga sky bug quits for this pass).

Add power to climb to and maintain 2500 feet. Take some left side views as you go. Presently a highway will appear on your windshield, and soon after you'll see the beginnings of a metropolitan area to the left of your course. The highway is I-580 and the city is Livermore. As the mountain on your left disappears off the windshield, a left front view will show you the beginnings of Lake Del Valle. You'll see only the northern end of the lake; your landing area is hidden by the mountain.

Just before you reach I-580, take a left side view. You should be able to see the whole of the Livermore metropolitan area, and the runway of Livermore Municipal just beyond it. Turn left to a heading of about 250 degrees and begin a descent. Then start improving your alignment for an eventual landing on Livermore's Runway 25. When you are closer, the airport layout will become more distinct. The runway is on the leftmost edge of the airport complex—the rest being ramp and taxiways. Knowing this should help guide you in if you've never landed at Livermore. Airport elevation is 405 feet.

You may want to pause a moment when the runway centerline and other details materialize. This is one of the finest airports the simulator offers. It's the only airport to date that features an actual tower structure. The ramp and taxiways are well defined. There's also a pilot shop with an accompanying fuel station. And finally, there's an ILS on the airport. You've probably been hearing and seeing its Outer and Middle Markers during your descent, though you're likely not tuned to the ILS frequency (110.5).

When you've landed, continue down the runway, then turn right and follow the outline of the taxiway around and onto the ramp area. Taxi behind the pilot shop and then come to a stop, parking between the shop and the tower.

If you're flying a version that offers a Tower view, here are parameters for the unique tower view in all the simulator world: Put the aircraft at N17303.893, E5250.4563, heading 162. Put the tower at N17303.978, E5249.9789, altitude 481 feet. This will give you a view of your aircraft through the tower windows. You can taxi to either runway, 07 or 25, in view of the tower all the way.

What's Buzzin'?

Chart: San Francisco
Title: WHATS BUZZIN?
En Route Coordinates:
  Aircraft: N17304, E5246
  Tower: N17303.978, E5249.9789
Altitude:
  Aircraft: 433
  Tower: 481
Heading: 053
Time: Daylight

Here's a classic buzzing scenario—another of those things you can't do in the real world. Come just as close to the tower here at Livermore Municipal as you dare.

If you have tower capability, you can watch your flyby from inside the tower, through the looking glass. You can decide if and when to veer off, if at all, based on what you see. Awesome indeed.

Long Way Across

Chart: San Francisco
Title: LONG WAY ACROSS
En Route Coordinates:
  Aircraft: N17423, E5056
  Tower: N17434.694, E5055.4641
Altitude:
  Aircraft: 588
  Tower: 15
Heading: 321
Time: Daylight

Flying under bridges is one thing. Flying across them, the long way, following the roadway, is quite another. And regardless of what you might see out your windshield as you cross the Golden Gate, *don't touch.*

Building Contract

Chart: San Francisco
Title: BLDG CONTRACT
En Route Coordinates:
　Aircraft: N17423, E5072
　Tower: ——
Altitude:
　Aircraft: 587
　Tower: ——
Heading: 135
Time: Daylight

This is another assignment from film director Steven Spielhof. A chopper is chasing you, and you are to fly between the twin sets of buildings straight ahead of you (the second two are very tough), then to the right of the next building you see (black in most versions). When you pass that building, bank left sharply and fly between the first two buildings that come into view. Then continue across San Francisco Bay and land on the little strip of green at the foot of Bay Bridge.

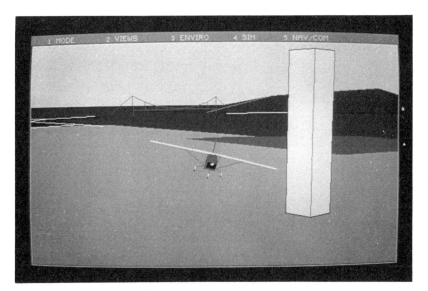

Golden Gate Bridge to the rear

Seeing you are a professional stunt pilot, you will certainly have checked out the elevation on that little patch of ground, but I'll remind you: It's 17 feet.

After you land, and with the chopper still chasing you, you jump out of the plane, run straight ahead, dive into the bay, and swim to the nearest point on the opposite shoreline. To enhance realism, the marksman firing at you from the chopper is, of course, using live ammunition.

Did you remember, by the way, to empty your pockets? In particular, did you put that advance paycheck in a safe place?

Mountaineering

Chart: San Francisco
Title: MOUNTAINEERING
En Route Coordinates:
   Aircraft: N17201, E5250
   Tower: N17183.709, E5165.6669
Altitude:
   Aircraft: 4855
   Tower: 139
Heading: 196
Time: Daylight

When you unpause, increase your power setting by about 200 rpm to hold your higher-than-usual initial altitude.

This scenario is purely for your enjoyment, flying in and around the Hamilton and Copernicus mountains southeast of San Jose, California.

As a suggestion, when you clear the ridge of Copernicus in the foreground, fly a bit to your left and cross Hamilton at the point between the peaks. (Rear Spot Plane views are great up here). You can lose some altitude between the mountains, but judge carefully. When you're approximately over the center of Hamilton, bank right steeply to a heading of about 290 and fly parallel to the ridge. Having some mountain in the foreground gives the whole landscape a feeling of depth. Then you can try a steep turn to the right, flying down the opposite slope toward the valley.

However you fly them, I hope you'll find mountains fun, a challenge, and exhilarating to explore.

A landing at San Jose suggests itself when you're finished. You can tune the San Jose VOR on 114.10 and center the OBI to find a heading, or just fly toward the buildings west of the mountains and you'll soon spot the airport out the right front. When the city disappears under you, turn right to a heading of 300 degrees and you'll be on a long final to Runway 30 Left, 30 Right, or just plain 29, which is the shorty of the bunch. Take your choice.

Like a Pro to SFO

Chart: San Francisco
Title: 115.8 INT R103
En Route Coordinates:
  Aircraft: N17371, E4980
  Tower: N17340.023, E5060.0702
Altitude:
  Aircraft: 1500
  Tower: 10/60 (Indefinite)
Heading: 009
Time: Day (Dusk or Night optional)
Special Requirements: Tune NAV 1 to 115.8 and set OBS to
                          R103

Here's a picturesque approach to San Franciso International, paralleling a right base along the Pacific coastline. The title reminds you of two specific things you must do in this scenario:

1. Tune NAV 1 to the San Francisco VOR, on a frequency of 115.80.
2. Set your OBS to radial 103, which you'll intercept and track to SFO (airport code, obviously, for San Francisco International).

This will set you up to execute a nice professional final approach.

The idea is to continue on your present heading while keeping a peeled eye on your OBI needle. After a few minutes, it will start moving toward the center of the instrument. When it does, observe the rate at which it moves—a rough analog of your distance from the station. The movement in this case is fairly rapid because you're only a dozen miles DME from your destination. Because you're crossing the radials rapidly, you'll want to start your turn to intercept R103 accordingly—that is, a few degrees ahead of the point where the needle will move to center.

Try to estimate this, and make your right turn to 103 degrees so you reach that heading just as the needle moves to center. Then fly the needle, which means do whatever you have to do to keep the OBI centered. The trick is to turn toward any deviation; that is, if the needle is to the right of center, yaw right a degree or two, if the needle is to the left of center, yaw left. When the needle is again centered, yaw to the heading indicated by the radial you're tracking, in this case 103 degrees. If that heading results in a "slippage" of the needle left or right, make a one-degree correction left or right. Your heading may not always agree exactly with the radial number; it could be a degree or so lower or higher. Accept such situations. As long as your compass heading and your selected radial are within a degree or so of agreement, fly the needle, regardless of what exact heading results. Keep the needle centered.

This tracking a VOR radial to a station is the primary means by which pilots the world over navigate from one section of a country to another, and finally to any destination airport. You could do this, using solely your instrument panel, if you had no outside references at all: no horizon, no landscape, no sky. You could do it in black of night, or socked in in an overcast. You don't have to know the names of towns, the lie of rivers, the destinations of highways, or anything else about the geography below you. All you need to know is the frequency of the VOR station to which you want to fly, and that your NAV radio is tuned to that frequency, that the radial you wish to track, and your present heading, are in virtual agreement, and that you're keeping the needle centered. Know those things, and you can navigate confidently to anywhere in the world you want to fly.

In the present case, radial 103 will point you straight to Runway 10 Left at San Francisco International, almost as accurately as would an ILS approach. The difference is that you have to decide what rate of descent, what "glideslope" will be required to touch down just beyond the runway threshold. (Your glideslope needle may become activated as in an ILS approach, but don't rely on it for this landing. Rely on your eyes.)

Enjoy your somewhat "classic" arrival at SFO.

Hangin' Around

Chart: San Francisco
Title: HANGING AROUND
En Route Coordinates:
  Aircraft: N17191, E5135
  Tower: N17220.561, E5134.9672
Altitude:
  Aircraft: 1500
  Tower: 8
Heading: 323
Time: Daylight

You are not on a landing approach to Moffett Naval Air Station. Instead, you're flying there to put on a benefit airshow for a big crowd of Californians. They've just caught sight of you, and are watching to see what you'll do.

Your first act should dazzle 'em. Glide down to a low altitude and fly through one of Moffett's three big blimp hangars—specifically, the first hangar to the right of the parallel runways.

If you have tower capability, be advised there's an observer at the other end of that hangar, ready to confirm that you touch neither the ground nor any part of the hangar.

The airshow is for the benefit of the WGOF (Wayward Girls Over Forty) Aid Society, so maybe you can take your expenses off your income tax.

CHAPTER FOUR
Scenery Disk 7

Washington Crossing

Chart: Washington
Title: WASHTN CROSSING
En Route Coordinates:
  Aircraft: N16853, E20825
  Tower: N16849.955, E20853.444
Altitude:
  Aircraft: 1500
  Tower: 218
Heading: 111
Time: Daylight

We'll enter southern New Jersey—and Scenery Disk 7—by crossing the Delaware River exactly where George Washington crossed it and, like Washington, we'll land in Trenton. But whereas Washington went there to do historic battle with the Hessians on Christmas Day (and defeat them) after a bitter winter encampment at Valley Forge, we go there to engage one of the simulator's shorter runways (Runway 11 is 2999 feet long), and see how well we do. (Note that Mercer County Airport has three runways, not one as shown on your chart.) You're on a long final approach.

Although Trenton is not one of America's most attractive capitals, it did play a grand role in history as the turning point of the American Revolution, and was once a candidate for capital of the United States.

Elevation at Mercer County is about 220 feet.

Do Not Pass Go

Chart: Washington
Title: DO NOT PASS GO
En Route Coordinates:
   Aircraft: N16471, E21053
   Tower: N16503.237, E20987.799
Altitude:
   Aircraft: 1500
   Tower: 80
Heading: 311
Time: Daylight

The water between you and Runway 31 at Atlantic City International is indeed the Atlantic Ocean, at Absecon Inlet. The beaches won't be crowded in Atlantic City this early in the year, but the casinos will be going full tilt. If, after you land, you go into town, you may want to walk the streets made famous by the board game Monopoly. It was invented here during the depression of the 1930s, and the avenues you buy and sell in the game are named after those of the real Atlantic City. The Miss America Pageant is held annually, of course, in Convention Hall, the largest building in the state. The famous eight-mile-long Boardwalk provides access to the many amusement piers, and you can still be pushed along it in the rolling chairs that were introduced here more than a hundred years ago. Elevation at ACY is 76 feet.

One final and personal note: Atlantic City was my destination on my first solo cross-country flight, from Totowa-Wayne Airport in northern New Jersey (that airport no longer exists). And guess what—I made it!

Delaware Cruise

Chart: Washington
Title: DELAWARE CRUISE
En Route Coordinates:
  Aircraft: N16780, E20869
  Tower: N16650.432, E20735.928
Altitude:
  Aircraft: 1600
  Tower: 21/218 (unreliable)
Heading: 251
Time: Daylight

Nothing like a long, winding river to establish a mood. You're over the Delaware at the point where it widens to become navigable south of Trenton. This river is second only to the Mississippi in annual tonnage carried. Unpause and follow it to Runway 27 at Philadelphia International.

You'll cross the Delaware River Turnpike Bridge (black line), which connects the New Jersey and Pennsylvania Turnpikes. New Jersey is on your left. Stay directly over the river. After it turns sharply right you'll see Northeast Philadelphia Airport on the west side of the water. The bridges to this side of the downtown Philadelphia buildings are the Tacony Palmyra and the Betsy Ross, and before you reach either of them you'll see PHL dead ahead. However, we're going to take the scenic route, so continue to follow the river.

Do, however, start a gradual descent to an approach altitude of 1000 feet.

Where the Delaware bends sharply left is the Ben Franklin Bridge, and after that is the Walt Whitman. Between these bridges, on the Jersey side, is the Camden metropolitan area. Camden was the last home and burial place of American poet and essayist Walt Whitman (1819–92). Even Walt might wonder what those buildings are doing, sticking up out of the water right next to his bridge.

Turn right with the river, then just a bit further right to a compass heading of 270—or whatever puts Runway 27 Left straight ahead of you—and proceed with your landing. Elevation at PHL is 26 feet.

Note: This flight is scenic at dawn or dusk, too.

A Rightful Base

Chart: Washington
Title: A RIGHTFUL BASE
En Route Coordinates:
  Aircraft: N16382, E20412
  Tower: N16366.078, E20379.495
Altitude:
  Aircraft: 1500
  Tower: 27
Heading: 228
Time: Day, Dawn, or Dusk

You're paralleling a right base leg for Runway 32 at Baltimore's Martin State Airport. *Paralleling* means you aren't in the airport traffic pattern proper, but a distance out. Still, you are on the heading you'd be on for a right base leg if you were in the pattern, and you'll make a right turn to your final approach—again, as you would if you were in the pattern. This could also be called a wide right base.

The scenario is a good one for practicing your turn to final. Exactly where you should start the turn depends on both your airspeed and the degree of bank you assume at the outset of the turn. Given an airspeed of 80–85 knots, and an approximate 30-degree bank and turn, try starting your turn when your destination runway is just forward of your wingtip (using a 90-degree right side view). Note that Runway 32 reaches right out to the water, which will help you identify it correctly; this will also help you not to start your turn too early.

Elevation at MTN is 24 feet.

Washington Courier

Chart: Washington
Title: WSHNGTN COURIER
En Route Coordinates:
   Aircraft: N16149, E20175
   Tower: N16151.109, E20194.893
Altitude:
   Aircraft: 1500
   Tower: 21
Heading: 101
Time: Daylight

What you are about to do is legal because you're an official air courier, and have important government documents aboard.

You have permission to land directly on the Washington Mall. Your landing area is well-delineated but circumscribed, so take a moment to study the following:

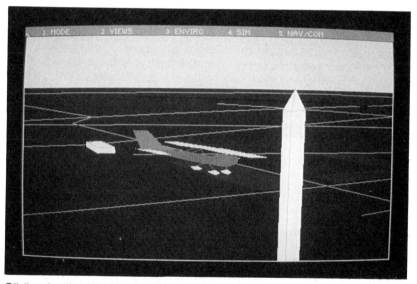

Gliding by the Washington Monument

The building well to the right of your course is the Pentagon. The rectangular area directly ahead, bounded by Constitution Avenue on the left and Independence Avenue on the right, is the Mall. At this end of the Mall is the Lincoln Memorial, which faces, across the Reflecting Pool, the Washington Monument. Just beyond the Washington Monument is 14th Street, dividing the Mall approximately in half.

You are to keep the Washington Monument well to your left, in a flight path that hugs Constitution Avenue. You will land on the grass on the other side of 14th Street. When you get closer, two additional roadways will appear: Madison Drive and Jefferson Drive. You are to land between Madison Drive and Constitution Avenue closer to Constitution Avenue. If you fly an approach too far left of Constitution Avenue, you'll see your intended landing area very late in the game, causing you to make energetic corrections. (This won't look too professional to workers in the Department of Agriculture, on whose front lawn you'll touch down.) Your landing should be executed at your lowest safe speed, using minimum throttle all the way for noise abatement purposes, and you'll apply your brakes promptly during the landing roll.

Got all that?

Then proceed according to plan. Elevation of the Mall is about 23 feet. When you are down, and while you await the messenger who will meet you and pick up your packet, you can admire the U.S. Capitol straight ahead of you. To the right of it are the House of Representatives offices. (Somewhere, well to your left on the other side of the Mall, are the offices of the Internal Revenue Service—but who could possibly care?)

Pentagonal Ploy

Chart: Washington
Title: PENTAGONAL PLOY
En Route Coordinates:
  Aircraft: N16140, E20184
  Tower: Same as previous
Altitude:
  Aircraft: 400
  Tower: Same as previous
Heading: 043
Time: Daylight

    This flyby will give you a closeup view of the Pentagon. One of the largest buildings in the world, it houses the complete administrative staffs of the entire U.S. military establishment.
    Note the lie of the Washington Monument in relation to your flight path, because after you pass over the Pentagon, you are to land again on that specific area of the Mall you studied in the last flight, with another delivery packet. Not as easy this time. (Use right side views to check out the area.)

Monumental Task

Chart: Washington
Title: MONUMENTAL TASK
En Route Coordinates:
  Aircraft: N16151, E20183
  Tower: ——
Altitude:
  Aircraft: 300
  Tower: ——
Heading: 099
Time: Daylight

You are pointed to fly straight over the Mall. The foreground building is the Lincoln Memorial, which faces the Reflecting Pool, then there's an open grassy area, and then the Washington Monument. At the far end of the Mall is the U.S. Capitol, atop Capitol Hill (which is why you hear politicians and newscasters refer to "the Hill.")

You'll likely need to execute an avoidance maneuver at the Washington Monument.

The Grecian-style Lincoln Memorial was opened in 1922. Inside it is a magnificent, oversize statue of the seated Lincoln, created by American sculptor Daniel Chester French. Though it looks as if it were carved from a single marble block, it actually consists of 28 separate sections.

The Washington Monument, a 555-foot-high masonry obelisk, was opened in 1888. It has 898 spiral steps—but, thankfully, you can take an elevator up.

The U.S. Capitol building was designed by an amateur in a contest in 1792, and George Washington himself laid the cornerstone a year later. (He chopped down the cherry tree. Beware your propeller doesn't chop down his monument.)

As you approach the Capitol, lose some altitude for a closeup look. The facade of the building is well-detailed in the simulation.

A Dawn Final to DCA 18

Chart: Washington
Title: DAWN FNL DCA 18
En Route Coordinates:
  Aircraft: N16189, E20183
  Tower: N16135.643, E20191.900
Altitude:
  Aircraft: 1500
  Tower: 19
Heading: 185
Time: Dawn (06:01)

This is one of my favorite dawn approaches in the Washington area. (I say "dawn," but I prefer to think of it as a night approach. In my opinion, as mentioned earlier in this book, dawn and dusk look more like night than does the simulator "night.")

You are on a long final to Runway 18 at Washington National Airport.

Your flight path is at a right angle to the Mall area, the western edge of which you'll cross. It takes you directly over the Lincoln Memorial. Just this side of the Mall is the Theodore Roosevelt Bridge, which touches down on the island of the same name as it crosses the Potomac River. At the foot of the bridge is the John F. Kennedy Center for the Performing Arts. Directly to the right of the Lincoln Memorial is the Arlington Memorial Bridge, crossing over to Arlington Cemetery. On the Mall just to the left and this side of the Lincoln Memorial is perhaps the most significant memorial of our times: the Vietnam Veterans Memorial. Though it is unseen in the simulation, let it not be unfelt.

You'll recognize the Pentagon on your right as you approach the double roadways of the George Mason Memorial Bridge. Mason, a Virginian and a patriot (1725–92), refused to sign the Constitution until it was enhanced with specific guarantees of individual rights.

Elevation at DCA is 24 feet.

Little Big Shot

Chart: Washington
Title: LITTLE BIG SHOT
En Route Coordinates:
  Aircraft: N16173, E19994
  Tower: N16161.432, E20043.312
Altitude:
  Aircraft: 1800
  Tower: 314
Heading: 119
Time: Daylight

At this distance you can get some idea of the giant, sprawling Dulles International Airport, on the Virginia side of the Potomac, one of the largest civil airports in the U.S. (if not the largest). Your approach is to the tiniest runway, 11 Left, in order that the 10,000-foot-plus runways can lie in readiness for the big jets. Runway 11L measures about 3000 by 75 feet.

John Foster Dulles, for whom the airport is named, had a distinguished career as a diplomat under Woodrow Wilson, FDR, and Harry Truman. He helped form the United Nations, and was Secretary of State under Dwight D. Eisenhower.

Elevation at Dulles is 319 feet. (The tower is near the threshold of Runway 11.)

An Artful Departure

Chart: Washington
Title: ARTFUL DEPART
Ground Coordinates:
  Aircraft: N16153 (16153.000), E20198 (20198.124)
  Tower: N16153.089, E20201.655
Altitude:
  Aircraft: 0
  Tower: 19
Heading: 104
Time: Daylight

Of course, as an official air courier, you have to have a flying area to depart from as well as land on when you carry messages to and from Washington. But they're not one and the same. You're looking at your departure "runway" now.

On your left is an important building virtually as handsomely detailed as the Capitol itself, the National Gallery of Art—also called The Mellon Gallery after Andrew Mellon who contributed the money to build it. It's one of the most prestigious art museums in the world. Take a good look at it early in your takeoff run.

Missing in the simulation, but located directly opposite the National Gallery of Art, is the giant Air and Space Museum that houses the Wright Brothers airplane, Charles A. Lindbergh's Spirit of St. Louis, the Apollo space capsule, and other air/space memorabilia.

This situation calls for a short takeoff, lest you violently disrupt a session of Congress or something. Pay close attention to what you're doing.

The Rappahannock River

Chart: Washington
Title: RAPPAHANNOCK R.
En Route Coordinates:
   Aircraft: N15780, E20283
   Tower: ——
Altitude:
   Aircraft: 1500
   Tower: ——
Heading: 149
Time: Daylight, Dawn or Dusk

In the hope that, like me, you love to track long, winding rivers across a countryside, I give you the long, beautiful reaches of Virginia's Rappahannock. This river is a smaller, more-or-less parallel companion of the Potomac. The Rappahannock runs into Chesapeake Bay like the Potomac, which is to the north of it.

I burden you with no anecdote, description, or history. A river is for unburdening.

Shifting Sands

Chart: Washington, then Charlotte
Title: SHIFTING SANDS
Ground Coordinates:
  Aircraft: N15055, E20628
  Tower: N15055.276, E20628.191
Altitude:
  Aircraft: 0
  Tower: 16
Heading: 151
Time: Daylight

You're pointed toward Runway 10 at Elizabeth City Coast Guard Air Station/Municipal Airport—obviously a double-duty facility—located in Elizabeth City, North Carolina. You'll find it at the bottom of your Washington Area Chart. Runway 10 isn't the one directly in front of you, as you can tell from your compass reading. You'll taxi ahead to the intersection and then turn left for your takeoff. This is a longer flight, so plan on your maximum cruise configuration.

Our destination is a revered place in aviation history— Kitty Hawk, North Carolina, the site, of course, of the first flight of the Wright brothers. As we fly there I'll give you a little background on those visionary bicycle repairmen, Wilbur and Orville.

This flight should be interesting for two more reasons. First, we're going to fly from one chart area to another, and sometimes that sort of transition will result in the aircraft being displaced by a few miles. It won't this time, however, if you fly carefully. Second, we're going to attempt a precision landing directly on Kitty Hawk, with very little to guide us (there's no airport there). So pay close attention, and follow my guidelines as carefully as you can.

When you're ready, taxi into position and take off. Climb straight out to 1000 feet, which will be our cruising altitude. Continue on the runway heading, 100 degrees, until you're over the last peninsula and see nothing but the Atlantic Ocean on your windshield. While you fly you'll have time to read the following capsule history.

Orville, the younger of the Wright brothers, was born in Dayton, Ohio in 1871. Wilbur was born near Millville, Indiana in 1867. Their first joint venture was publishing a small weekly newspaper. The bicycle repair business was the second.

The brothers developed a passion for the sport of gliding, having read of the experiments of Germany's Otto Lilienthal who made hundreds of flights. Lilienthal's technique for controlling the equilibrium of his gliders was to shift the weight of his body, a flawed procedure that resulted in his death in 1896. The Wrights developed a far more sophisticated technique, in which the center of gravity remained constant and equilibrium was controlled by adjusting the angles of the wings and other airfoils, thus varying the air pressure against them. They patented their system, and you experience it today as aileron and elevator control.

Their interest in gliding soon gave way to study of the serious scientific aspects of aeronautics. Because they found the existing data unsatisfactory, they abandoned it and did their own investigating. They created a small wind tunnel in which they could measure the lift and drag of a wide variety of airfoils and airfoil combinations, a pursuit that interested them so intensely that they often worked at it around the clock.

Believing their data now made it possible to predict the performance of a flying machine—one that would require far less power than had been proposed up until that time—they set about in October of 1902 to design and build an engine-driven aircraft. When completed a little more than a year later, their machine weighed 750 pounds complete with Orville as pilot. Its four-cylinder engine developed just 12 horsepower. But that was sufficient to permit Orville to take off and fly for 59 seconds at a speed of 30 mph. The plane made four such flights on December 17, 1903, over distances as short as 120 feet and as long as 852 feet. The rest, as they say, is history. By 1906 they were able to stay aloft for an hour or more.

When only ocean is visible ahead, turn right and fly a compass heading of 170 degrees. You'll be flying along the eastern edge of a barrier island, which looks almost rectangular seen from the cockpit, though your map will confirm it's shaped more like an arrowhead.

After some minutes, the land you're flying over abruptly narrows. Your course should take you over the center of the narrow portion, and as you come to it, an airport will appear about 10 degrees to the right of your heading. That's Dare County Regional Airport, Manteo, North Carolina. At this point, slow the airplane down and drop your gear.

Take a look straight back. The near edge of the wider portion of the barrier island will come into view to the right of your horizontal stabilizer. Keep the rear view, and when you can see the whole of the wide section of island outlined against the water, restore your out-front view and do a gentle 180 to the right (use half your usual bank, or about 15 degrees, for a gradual turn), rolling out on a heading of about 340, or so the wide section of island is straight ahead of you.

Now land straight ahead, treating the geography at the edge of the water as if it were the threshold of a runway. Elevation is about 20 feet. Use flaps if required, trying to land just beyond the water's edge. When you're on the ground, put on your brakes.

You can't see them, but you're surrounded by sand dunes and, perhaps, by ghostly wings. You're there. Where it happened. Kitty Hawk.

Enable your map. The white spot behind you is Manteo/Dare County Regional Airport. Just to the right of the airport, across the water, at the thinnest part of the island, is Kill Devil Hills. There, rather than on Kitty Hawk proper, is the sand dune area where the Wright Brothers National Memorial stands. The reason the sites of the memorial and of the actual historic flight are different is that the contours of this area have changed over time. This island and its dunes are continually reshaped by wind and wave, and the location of both Kitty Hawk and Kill Devil Hills is not what it was in the time of the Wright brothers. So no one can point to a specific spot today and say "Exactly there . . ."

But the whole area is memorialized by what happened at Kitty Hawk. And at Dare County airport there's a VOR station, aptly named Wright Brothers.

The Lost Colony

Chart: Charlotte
Title: LOST COLONY/MQI
En Route Coordinates:
  Aircraft: N14952, E20803
  Tower: N14924.085, E20818.230
Altitude:
  Aircraft: 800
  Tower: 18
Heading: 160
Time: Daylight

The rough rectangle of land in front of you is Roanoke Island, North Carolina, and you're positioned for a long final to Runway 16 at Dare County Airport, Manteo, North Carolina (airport code MQI).

Before you unpause to fly the approach, however, take a hard look at the near tip of the island. See if you see any sign of life. Because in 1587, Sir Walter Raleigh started a colony down there, consisting of 117 settlers led by a mysterious man named John White. He may have been the artist John White, painter of invaluable historic watercolors of southeastern Indian life and of native plants and animals. Or he may have been some other John White. At any rate, because the supplies of these early settlers were in danger of running out, John White made a voyage to England for more provisions. But when he returned three years later there was absolutely no trace of the colonists, no indication whatsoever that they had ever been there. Even the fort they had built had vanished. The only sign of any life was the word "Croatoan" (the name of a local Indian tribe) carved on a tree. But had the Croatoan committed some hostile act, it seems unlikely that any settler would have had the time to carve Croatoan on a tree. At any rate, to this day no one knows what became of The Lost Colony, commemorated today as the Fort Raleigh National Historic Site. The fort has been rebuilt, and a drama, *The Lost Colony*, is enacted for tourists at Waterside Theater during the summer months.

Dare County Airport resembles an asterisk from the air. Elevation is 13 feet (and a ground observer is alongside the threshold end of Runway 16).

Cape Hatteras

Chart: Charlotte
Title: CAPE HATTERAS
En Route Coordinates:
  Aircraft: N14641, E20993
  Tower: N14486.042, E20415.374
Altitude:
  Aircraft: 1500
  Tower: 24
Heading: 274
Time: Dawn (06:01)
Special Requirements: See text

You're approaching Cape Hatteras, North Carolina. And yes, "There's a lighthouse by the sea." (Anyone know that old song?) Imagine how welcome that light would be if you'd just flown the Atlantic, or for that matter sailed it.

Cape Hatteras has been called the "graveyard of the Atlantic" because so many ships in the throes of Atlantic storms were wrecked on its coast. Game fishermen here work the outer banks for tuna, sailfish and blue marlin, but bathers and sunbathers simply enjoy the beaches.

You have alternatives for this scenario. You can proceed to make an improvised landing right on the Cape (with a close look at Hatteras Light on your way down). Or if you'd prefer an extended flight, continue on your present course (you'll still get a good look at the lighthouse as you fly over it). The Cape Hatteras National Seashore will be off to your left, and you'll fly over Pamlico Sound toward the North Carolina coast. Advance the time an hour for a better view of things. (Take a look out the left rear before you've flown too far, and you may find that the Hatteras lamp is still lit—there's a 50-50 chance.) As you come up on the shoreline, turn left to a heading of 245 degrees, or tune and track the New Bern VOR on 113.60, and fly down to Simmons-Nott Airport, where you'll cross the Neuse River and land on Runway 22. If you elect this extended trip, be prepared for a rather lengthy but pleasant flight.

Tobacco Road

Chart: Charlotte
Title: 117.2 INT R230
En Route Coordinates:
  Aircraft: N14887, E19712
  Tower: N14767.990, E19771.000
Altitude:
  Aircraft: 1500
  Tower: 441
Heading: 129
Time: Daylight, Dawn, or Dusk
Special Requirements: Tune NAV 1 to 117.20. Set OBS to
                         R230

Proceed with your flight, transitioning to maximum cruise configuration if you wish.

You're over the northwestern end of a spiny body of water called the Lake of the Neuse Reservoir. Your present course will take you just beyond it before, with your NAV tuned and OBS set as described above, you intercept radial 230, turn to track the needle, and begin a long final approach to Runway 23 at Raleigh-Durham Airport, Raleigh, North Carolina.

In the country to all sides of your course, tobacco is the money crop. A bit east of here, true, they grow cotton, corn, vegetables, soybeans and peanuts, and they raise hogs. But tobacco is still the major crop, and from here west to Greensboro and Winston-Salem it's virtually the only crop.

When you've turned final, it's time to slow the airplane and get your gear down. But don't lose altitude too fast. Raleigh-Durham's elevation is 437 feet, so you're virtually at pattern altitude at 1500.

If you were wondering, Raleigh is the metropolitan area to your left, and Durham is to your right. U.S. 70 and I-40 connect them. Just beyond the airport you'll see a bit of B. Everette Jordan Lake.

The capitol at Raleigh, by the way, was originally located just four miles from a bistro named Hunter's Tavern, an alternate location having been rejected because it was 10 miles from said tavern, thus too far to go for a drink.

Doin' the Charleston

Chart: Charleston
Title: THE CHARLESTON
En Route Coordinates:
  Aircraft: N13385, E19457
  Tower: N13365.889, E19459.717
Altitude:
  Aircraft: 1200
  Tower: 24
Heading: 181
Time: Daylight

That's our runway, that little one tucked way over in the corner. Runway 18—although it isn't documented and doesn't show up on the charts—is a runway all the same, and it's at Charleston Executive Airport, Charleston, South Carolina. Our landing there will put us in reach of the city where the Civil War began, and where Porgie and Bess lived, too, and more.

It was the explosion of a confederate shell on the parade ground of Fort Sumter on April 12, 1861 that started the war. The fort—actually a giant raft of stone and brick, and now a national monument—is in Charleston Harbor, which you can see out your left-side and rear windows.

Charleston is also the birthplace of the play *Porgie and Bess,* by DuBose Heyward, later turned into the famous opera by that author and George and Ira Gershwin. The name Porgy was derived from the fish peddlers Heyward heard chanting "Porgiee!" along Catfish Row, known in Charleston as Cabbage Row. It was there that Harlem dope peddler Sportin' Life's "happy dust" led to murder, lust, and temptation, and where the soulful story of love, loss and the crippled Porgy's forlorn love unfolded.

More recently, Charleston was the birthplace of the magnificent theme song of the civil rights movement, *We Shall Overcome,* based on a hymn Charleston's blacks found in a white Baptist hymnal and sang during a 1946 food and tobacco workers' strike.

Elevation at Charleston Executive is about 20 feet.

Blinking Beautiful

Chart: Jacksonville
Title: BLINKNG BEAUTFL
En Route Coordinates:
  Aircraft: N12325, E19051
  Tower: ——
Altitude:
  Aircraft: 967
  Tower: ——
Heading: 285
Time: Dawn (06:01)
Special Requirements: If, due to pausing or other factors, the time gets close to 06:30 as you follow this scenario, turn the clock back to retain the dawn lighting throughout the flight and landing.

Each Scenery Disk introduces one or more scenic touches we haven't seen before in the simulator. The Cape Hatteras Lighthouse was one in Scenery Disk 7. Here in Jacksonville, Florida, as we follow the St. Johns River into and through the city, you'll see another that is, to be precise, just what the title says—blinking beautiful.

Proceed with your flight, staying over the center of the river. Other than a little glimpse of Craig Municipal Airport well to the left on your windshield, there isn't much to see until you make that first left turn where the St. Johns does. Then you see more of Craig, and you also see—blinking transmitter towers! Somehow, for me, these towers (and there are more of them) make the dawn landscape come alive, and make Jacksonville a believable as well as beautiful metropolitan area.

Before you get to the next bend of the river, you see another tower, and then another, plus, though at a distance, the only building simulated in Jacksonville. And as you bank right with the river, still another tower is revealed in the second group.

When your heading is in the 260s somewhere, and there are three towers on the left side of your windshield, the river ahead will appear to turn left. But it doesn't, as you can see by looking out the left side. So continue straight ahead until the next "corner," where the river gets wider, and follow it around to the right. The airport visible to the right of your course now is Jacksonville International.

Take a look out the left side, and when a couple of the transmitter towers are under your wingtip, turn left and fly toward the cluster of three towers, keeping the solitary building straight ahead. Shortly you'll see that the two leftmost towers are on opposite sides of the river. Just before the near shore of the St. Johns passes under your nose, turn right to a heading of 250–255 degrees, so Herlong Airport is straight ahead of you. A lone blinking tower signals your final approach to Runway 25, elevation 96 feet. As you go, a larger airport will put in an appearance beyond Herlong—Cecil Field Naval Air Station. But you're for Herlong 25.

Jacksonville Executive

Chart: Jacksonville
Title: JAX EXECUTIVE
Ground Coordinates:
  Aircraft: N12282, E18946
  Tower: N12282.046, E18936.132
Altitude:
  Aircraft: 0
  Tower: 27
Heading: 115
Time: Daylight, Dawn or Dusk

You might like to have a private airport here in Jacksonville, so I give you Jacksonville Executive, in the heart of downtown, with its landing area well-defined, and with a view of three blinking transmitter towers to light your way. How do you like that?

Named for Andrew Jackson, Jacksonville is the largest city in Florida. Indeed, in area (827 square miles), it's the largest in the world. It served as a Confederate base in the Civil War and, though 20 miles from the Atlantic Ocean, developed into a major deepwater port. The British composer Frederick Delius (1862–1934) made his home here on what is now the Jacksonville College campus; the house has been restored and is open to visitors.

I'm sure you'll want to try out your new airport, so take off and fly around a bit. Then try to get into a good approach position and land back here again. Note your compass and altimeter readings before you go.

Downwind For Same

Chart: Jacksonville
Title: DWNWND JAX EXEC
En Route Coordinates:
　　Aircraft: N12287, E18947
　　Tower: Same as previous
Altitude:
　　Aircraft: 920
　　Tower: Same as previous
Heading: 295
Time: Optional

　　You can fly a standard airport pattern for Jacksonville Executive, as this scenario shows. You are downwind and approximately opposite your intended landing point. Proceed to fly the rest of the pattern, but land wherever on the area you feel like landing. I like to make my approach well to the right of our takeoff position, so I have the building in view all or most of the way down (you can even cross the building's shadow on your rollout). Your base leg heading is, of course, about 205 degrees (downwind minus 90, or final plus 90, whichever way you want to read it).

Other Way To Go

Chart: Jacksonville
Title: OTHER WAY TO GO
En Route Coordinates:
  Aircraft: N12277, E18961
  Tower: Same as previous
Altitude:
  Aircraft: 800
  Tower: Same as previous
Heading: 295
Time: Optional

Here you're on final for Jacksonville Executive from the other direction, landing toward the St. Johns River. Your landing area, remember, is beyond the point where the highways join. And you should be approximately opposite the building when you touch down. (This approach is a beauty when observed or replayed with the tower view.)

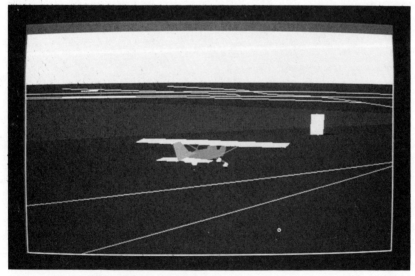

The airport in the distance has tower

Impromptu

Chart: Jacksonville
Title: IMPROMPTU-C KEY
Ground Coordinates:
  Aircraft: N12255, E17942
  Tower: N12254.549, E17936.397
Altitude:
  Aircraft: 0
  Tower: 86
Heading: 350
Time: Daylight

There's a little island and fishing village called Cedar Key in the Gulf of Mexico. Get out your chart and eyeball a line due south from the Cross City VOR compass rose. The line will cross a river, the Suwannee, and then intersect a little bump of mainland. Just below the bump you'll see a dot in the Gulf. That's Cedar Key.

My idea for this scenario is to fly to Cedar Key, following the Gulf coastline, and put the airplane down somewhere on that dot. I haven't done it, and I don't know if we can do it, or whether Cedar Key is even simulated. But I want to try it. You with me?

The threshold for the active runway, 27, is just ahead, and we're cleared to taxi into position and take off. Your maximum cruise configuration is called for on this flight.

Climb out to 500 feet on the runway heading and then turn left to 150 degrees. We'll cruise at 1500 feet. When you're at that altitude you'll have your first view of the Gulf of Mexico (at least in *Odyssey*).

Shortly you'll see two rivers—the Aucilla and the Wacissa—joining to flow together into the Gulf. When you're over the big water, fly a heading of 125 degrees, keeping the shoreline to your left.

Tallahassee (which we just departed in case you were wondering) is the capital city of Florida. Most of the land you can see to your left is uncultivated forest and swampland, but there's good fishing in the Gulf waters, particularly for red snapper, mullet and grouper.

Florida has the longest coastline of any state except Alaska. The Gulf and Atlantic Ocean coastlines together add

73

up to 1350 miles. Wherever you might be in the Sunshine State, you are never more than 100 miles from the sea.

The shoreline is quite uneven, but just average it. A heading of about 145 should do nicely. Out the left side and on your map you can see that you're paralleling a highway, Alt U.S. 27, which is also U.S. 19 and U.S. 98. It should be possible to spot Foley Airport along the way, but I haven't seen it so far. And the next airport checkpoint will be Cross City, after which spotting the Suwannee River will be critical to our identifying and confirming Cedar Key. (If, again, you've been wondering, yes, the Suwannee is the river Stephen Foster had in mind in *Old Folks At Home,* though in fact he never laid eyes on it.)

Just as I finished writing the line above, I see the river ahead. Almost at the same moment, Cross City is visible out the left side, though it virtually merges with the highway.

When you know you have the river spotted, point to cross it exactly at the shoreline where the river meets the Gulf. Then, as you cross the triangular island formed by the mouths of the river, yaw right to a heading of about 160 degrees. That's what I'm doing, and that should point us to Cedar Key if the chart is reasonably accurate, and if the island is really there.

And indeed there is what appears to be an island out there. My heading at the moment is 158 degrees. And yes, I can see Cedar Key on my map, too.

I suggest we fly around the island first, and take stock of the landing possibilities. When you get near it, fly to the right of it, heading about 175 degrees. Get it off your left wingtip and then fly a wide-ranging turn-around-a-point, using a gentle bank that keeps the island constantly in view out the left side. If it moves toward the rear, steepen the bank a bit. Practice holding the island precisely where you want it under your wingtip.

Cedar Key looks easily big enough to accommodate a landing in any of several directions on its triangular shape. The base (of the triangle) runs 90 degrees to the shoreline, and I vote we land along the base, and to the northeast—in other words toward the shore. Why? Because that's the shortest side, and I know you like the toughest possible assignments. The "runway," then, is on a bearing of, say, 50 degrees, so we'll call it Runway 05.

Wherever you are now, slow down, get your gear down, and start thinking in pattern terms. Where are you in relation to Runway 05? Just how will you fly a pattern that puts you on final for that runway? Do your arithmetic and your other skullwork and go ahead and land. Then come back and I'll tell you what I did.

(I don't know the elevation here, but I'd assume it's something around 25 feet.)

I was east and north of the island and upwind, heading 045 degrees, when I wrote the foregoing two paragraphs. I slowed down, dropped my gear, and started losing some altitude. Then I turned left (crosswind, heading 320) and watched the island pass by out the left side. When it was a little to the rear of my left wingtip, I turned downwind, heading 230 degrees, and again examined the landing area out the left side, imagining a runway along the edge of the water. I extended the downwind leg to give myself plenty of time to turn base (140 degrees) and final (050 degrees) and get lined up. Figuring I had plenty of runway length, but not knowing the field elevation, I made a slow, flat airline approach, using just 10 degrees of flaps.

I landed uneventfully and came to a stop about halfway up the "strip." I checked the altimeter, and found the elevation was about 89 feet—considerably higher than my guess. I had hoped to be closer to the shore, but played it safe so I wouldn't wind up in the drink.

Speaking of which, I could use one.

But isn't an improvised landing like that, on an unknown bit of geography, beautiful to fly? And where else but in the simulator could we do it?

This little village is famous for seafood, so in your honor we'll go to a seafood restaurant. But I have to tell you that the only seafood I eat is oysters and canned tuna. Right now I'd give you all the lobster and shrimp in the world for one good tunafish sandwich.

Gentlemen, Start . . .

Chart: Jacksonville
Title: GENTLEMEN,START
En Route Coordinates:
  Aircraft: N11788, E19252
  Tower: N11807.159, E19214.510
Altitude:
  Aircraft: 1200
  Tower: 40
Heading: 330
Time: Daylight

Start your engines, of course. We're inbound to Daytona Beach Regional, home of the Daytona International Speedway, of Daytona 500 and Firecracker 400 fame. Years ago, auto land speed records were set here—not on the speedway, but on the city's wide, sandy beaches (you can get an idea of them below you). Today, you can still drive a car on some parts of the beach, but the speed limit is a less-than-thrilling 10 mph.

You're paralleling a long base leg, to be followed by a not-so-long final, for Runway 24 Left—shortest of the airport's strips. Elevation is 35 feet.

Come On Down

Chart: Jacksonville
Title: COME ON DOWN
En Route Coordinates:
  Aircraft: N11618, E19340
  Tower: N11568.417, E19360.943
Altitude:
  Aircraft: 10000
  Tower: 14
Heading: 130
Time: Daylight
Special Requirements: See text

Study the landscape far below you carefully. The diagonal line visible at the bottom right of your windshield is the Shuttle Landing Facility. You have re-entered the atmosphere in the space shuttle, and are to glide to a landing on that facility, on a compass heading of 150 degrees—on Runway 15.

There are two things you must do before you begin: First, since you have no power in the space shuttle, back your throttle off to idle; and second, for the same reason, disable the simulator sound (check your manual for how to do this in your version).

Birds-eye view of the pads

Now, remembering you have no power, but have considerable altitude to lose, you'll unpause and glide to your landing.

The first thing to do is apply some up elevator because the airplane wants to descend steeply in its present configuration. The nose will come up and your airspeed will drop (try to keep it below 80 knots). Your elevator now controls both your airspeed and your rate of descent, and they are tradeoffs of each other. Your job is to stay in control all the way, turning, circling, flying straight, correcting your rate of descent and your moment-to-moment heading—in other words, doing whatever you have to do to suit your relationship to the runway. Keep the runway in sight as much as possible—all the time if you can.

When you get to a lower altitude, you'll see that the Shuttle Landing Facility has a centerline. And best of all, this landing strip is 17000—yes 17000—feet long, and 350 feet wide. Talk about margin for error.

You have an additional aid in making this approach: your flaps. Use them if you need them, and when and where they'll do the most good. They'll increase drag, but will lower the aircraft's stalling speed. They'll also permit a steeper descent without undue increase in airspeed.

Put the whole thing together to the best of your ability. Just remember that you have no throttle, and suppress the urge to use it. No fair if you do use it.

If you keep your airspeed low, you'll be amazed at how much time you have to "prepare" this approach and landing. Elevation at the threshold of Runway 15 is just shy of 17 feet (I measured it in place).

Good luck.

Launch Complex 39A

Chart: Jacksonville
Title: LAUNCH CMPLX 39
En Route Coordinates:
  Aircraft: N11573, E19389
  Tower: ——
Altitude:
  Aircraft: 133
  Tower: ——
Heading: 009
Time: Daylight

You're looking, not simply at a shuttle on its launch pad, but at a National Historic Site: Launch Complex 39A. If you look at your map and adjust the zoom, you'll see the site is surrounded by a circular road. Just north is a similar site, though empty. It's also surrounded by a circular road, is a part of the same National Historic Site, and is Launch Complex (you guessed it) 39B. The body of water between the two launch pads is known as Gator Hole. Behind the complex is the Banana River, and ahead of it (you may have to adjust zoom) you'll see Mosquito Lagoon, separated from the Atlantic by a thin strip of seashore that forms a boundary for both John F. Kennedy Space Center and a Wildlife Refuge. The little bump of land southeast of the complex is known as False Cape, the true Cape Canaveral being south of there.

To the left you can see the Shuttle Landing Facility where you made your magnificent landing on the last flight. The road paralleling the runway is Kennedy Parkway, which leads to Launch Control Center and another circular road. Just left of the Parkway, south of the runway, is Banana Creek, a tributary of the Indian River.

Now that you're familiar with this part of the Kennedy Space Center, it's time to get familiar with the shuttle on its launch pad.

Let me tell you something, and you'll have to take my word for it. It is possible to fly between the shuttle and the launch tower from where you are. But your judgment must be unimpaired when you try it. Not only must your heading be precise, but your altitude is critical—and you must judge both of these visually. In particular, you must be at an altitude that will clear the base of the launch pad, but be below the gantry arms. You'll be flying through a little square slot.

Perhaps, the first time, you'd rather just sightsee the shuttle, in which case you should bank a bit to your right before flying by it, and take views out the left side.

Then, maybe the second time . . .

Play Nine Pins

Chart: Jacksonville
Title: PLAY NINE PINS
En Route Coordinates:
    Aircraft: N11540, E19408
    Tower: ——
Altitude:
    Aircraft: 110
    Tower: ——
Heading: 155
Time: Daylight

Yes, there are nine of those rocket gantry towers and, un-
like the shuttle in the prior scenario, if you hit any part of
them you'll know it.

You're to fly to the left of the first tower, then to the
right of the second, to the left of the third, and so on, until
you've cleared all nine. At that point you'll be over the true
Cape Canaveral, where you'll set the airplane down (this side
of the Atlantic, of course).

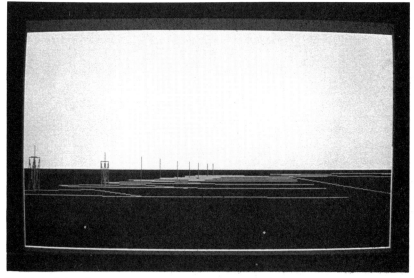

Florida's flying freeway

Remember what you've learned watching slalom skiers (except they hit the markers and you can't). Use any and all devices and techniques that come to mind (rudder can be very useful, if not indispensable). Watch your altitude, too. You're low at the outset, and will likely lose altitude in the turns. If your wheels touch the ground, you're disqualified.

All set?

Go.

Top Secret Base

Chart: Jacksonville
Title: TOP SECRET BASE
En Route Coordinates:
 Aircraft: N11536, E19272
 Tower: ——
Altitude:
 Aircraft: 1500
 Tower: ——
Heading: 274
Time: Daylight

   Tell you what. There are what sure look like rocket gan-try towers out there. There are even nine of them. Even at this distance you can count them. But I'll tell you something else: That isn't the Kennedy Space Center, and its nowhere near Cape Canaveral. You're well west of both. If you check your map, you'll see the Cape area and the ocean are far behind you.

   So what are those rocket gantry towers doing out there in the middle of Florida swampland? Have we stumbled on a secret rocket installation? Is this some kind of camouflage, or a trick done with mirrors? There's only one way to find out. I recommend we fly straight ahead and land just this side of the towers for a closer look. That may solve the mystery.

   So, unpause and do just that. We'll continue this conversation when we're parked down there by the towers.

Big Town

Chart: Miami
Title: L BASE TPA 09
En Route Coordinates:
  Aircraft: N11280, E18667
  Tower: N11238.592, E18685.959
Altitude:
  Aircraft: 1500
  Tower: 29
Heading: 180
Time: Daylight

As the title for SAVE purposes indicates, you're on an extended left base for Runway 09 at Tampa International. And what a vista! Only fitting for western Florida's sprawlingest town, where they brew beer, manufacture cigars in the country's biggest cigar factory, and export more phosphate than any port in the world. In addition, Tampa is a major hub for the citrus industry, was a shipbuilding center in World War II, and is home of Florida's biggest shrimp fleet. Finally, just south of town is MacDill, one of the nation's largest Air Force bases.

That blaze of light ahead isn't highways, but bridges. We'll see more of them in the next couple of scenarios.

For now, proceed with your approach to Runway 09, shortest strip on Tampa International. Elevation is 34 feet.

Bridges Very Far

Chart: Miami
Title: BRDGES VERY FAR
Ground Coordinates:
  Aircraft: N11239 (11239.413), E18695 (18694.479)
  Tower: N11205.159, E18630.553 (at destination)
Altitude:
  Aircraft: 0
  Tower: 14
Heading: 308 (272)
Time: Daylight

Did I remember to thank you for letting me stop off at Orlando, so I could visit Walt Disney World and get my Mickey Mouse t-shirt? How do you think it looks on me?

No, I'm not sorry I asked.

On this flight we'll take a good look at the Tampa-St. Petersburg area from the air. This is a fine section of Florida for local flights, with its bridges and causeways, intricately shaped shorelines, and numerous airports with over-water approaches. We'll cover many miles (don't undertake this flight unless and until you're in the mood for a long one), but we'll land only a short distance from here, at St. Petersburg's Clearwater International.

We're cleared for takeoff on Runway 27, so proceed.

As you climb out you'll see the Courtney Campbell Causeway off to your left, paralleling the shore. A little distance ahead it bends to the left. Follow the causeway, which connects Tampa and Clearwater across Old Tampa Bay. Plan to level off at 1000 feet.

Note that this structure has a centerline, and casts a shadow.

Keep going straight ahead when the causeway ends, and fly to the far shore and a bit out over the Gulf of Mexico, until you see no shoreline if you take a view directly down. Then turn left to a heading of about 183 degrees.

Out the left side now is Clearwater International. Ahead and to your left you'll see what looks like a string of islands. At the near end are Redington Beach and Madeira Beach. Farther south are Treasure Island, Long Key, and St. Petersburg Beach. The bay they create is Boca Chiega Bay. As you cross it, about where it meets the Gulf, turn left and head 150 degrees. You'll be flying along the island chain toward the big curve of the Sunshine Skyway Bridge.

Continue across lower Tampa Bay, still heading 150, and keeping the long, sweeping bridge a little to your left. On your right will be a boomerang-shaped island, Mullet Key, where Fort DeSoto is located. It's best seen out the right front and side when you're nearly opposite it. Straight ahead of you, on the far shore, is Bradenton, Florida.

As the shoreline disappears under the aircraft's nose, turn left to a heading of about 100 degrees, or until the Sunshine Skyway Bridge (it's really two bridges, side by side) is just visible on the left edge of your windshield. It will disappear momentarily, but keep flying, observing the lie of the bridge out the left front and then the left side. When the parallel roadways leading to the bridges are under your left wingtip, enter a 30-degree bank and turn to the left, to whatever heading puts the visual center of the two bridges at the center of your windshield. The idea is to get over one bridge or the other, or over the water between them, as or before they depart the shoreline. Then, just track the roadways.

This is surely an unusual pair of bridges. One wonders why it was feasible to build two narrow ones rather than one wide one. But there must have been a good reason. Follow them to shore.

When you reach the shore, continue straight ahead, but set up a 500- foot-per-minute descent to an altitude of 200 feet. When you have that altitude, adjust your power to hold it. Meanwhile, correct your heading if necessary to point to the near end of the roadway leading to the first bridge you see ahead: the Gandy Bridge. The near highway, Interstate 275, leads straight to it. (Those towers, by the way, are transmitter towers, and they blink in the non-daylight hours like those in Jacksonville.)

You'll turn right to follow the roadway leading to the bridge. But your perspective can be deceiving at this altitude, so enter the turn with some care or you may overshoot. In any event, correct as needed to fly directly above the roadway.

Mind your altitude, and follow this bridge over Old Tampa Bay. (I have a feeling all highways may look like this in the simulator one day—but without the shadow, of course—rather than being just pencil-thin lines.) This is probably the most unusual over-water flight in all the simulator world.

When you reach the opposite shore, turn toward the building you'll see well to the left on your screen. Fly to the right of the building (at this altitude you sure can't fly over it) and note that it has a shadow that, when analyzed, says it's morning here in Tampa, despite whatever your clock may read.

We have one more bridge to fly over: the Howard Franklin. This one will take us to our landing at Clearwater International. When you've passed the building with the shadow, start climbing for an altitude of about 1000 feet and make a long turn to your left, to a heading of about 245 degrees, keeping Tampa International to your right. The far side of the Howard Franklin Bridge should be straight ahead, and just to the right of it you'll see Clearwater Airport. It has a Runway 27, and that's where you'll set her down. Approximately where the bridge jogs left, you'll jog right, and be in perfect position for your final approach.

Elevation is 11 feet.

Keep Left

Chart: Miami
Title: KEEP LEFT
En Route Coordinates:
    Aircraft: N11188, E18656
    Tower: ——
Altitude:
    Aircraft: 784
    Tower: ——
Heading: 072
Time: Daylight

You're about to make one of the most unusual landings
you've ever made in the simulator—perhaps the most unusual.

Obviously, you're going to attempt a landing on the
roadway of Gandy Bridge. That's a bit unusual in itself because there aren't many roadways like this in the simulator.
But that's just the beginning of what's unusual about this scenario.

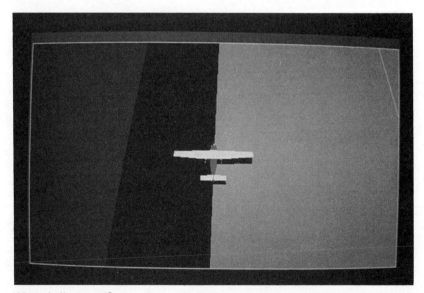

Where's the road?

I don't want to reveal the whole story yet. So don't read beyond this paragraph. Go ahead and shoot your landing. Then you'll be ready for the unfolding of the whole mystery of Gandy Bridge. Proceed to land, and only then read on. . . .

*   *   *

There are two fascinating aspects to this roadway. If you landed successfully on it (or thought you did) you've surely discovered the first one: The roadway is utterly without substance. As I don't have to tell you, you sank right through the pavement to the water below . . . or onto the bridge's shadow. If you got the SPLASH message, you hit the water, either on landing or during the landing roll. If, however, you didn't get the SPLASH message, you landed and stayed on the roadway's shadow, and Fascinating Aspect Number Two was revealed to you: The shadow supported you and your aircraft. As the French say, incredible!

The title of this scenario, "Keep Left," reveals the secret of landing on Gandy without a SPLASH. If you land on the left side of the roadway, the shadow will be under you when you touch down and you won't get a soaking. In fact, you even have time between sinking through the pavement and touching down to yaw the aircraft so the wheels hit the shadow if you're about to miss it. Then if you're agile at steering, you can stay on the shadow and . . . mission accomplished!

If you SPLASHed, try the scenario again—as many times as necessary—until you land safely on the shadow. This allows you to have some more fun, as follows:

Make your normal takeoff, using the Gandy shadow as a runway. You'll climb right through the roadway into the sunlight, without so much as a scratch on your airplane.

Gone Fishin'

Chart: Miami
Title: 112.4 INT R170
En Route Coordinates:
  Aircraft: N10826, E19266
  Tower: N10770.054, E19428.881
Altitude:
  Aircraft: 1500
  Tower: 20
Heading: 090
Time: Daylight (Dawn/Dusk Optional)
Special Requirements: Tune NAV 1 112.40, set OBS R170

Spread ahead of you is Florida's largest lake, Lake Okeechobee. The finger of land is known as Observation Shoal and is, like much of the country hereabouts, marshland. Not far behind you, however, are lush forests, grazing lands for livestock, sugar cane plantations, and the inevitable Florida citrus groves.

You're pointed at the approximate center of this giant but very shallow lake, famous for bass fishing and, when the largemouths aren't biting, crappie, redear and bluegill.

Your NAV should be tuned to the Pahokee VOR on 112.40, and Radial 170 set on your OBS. Your DME shows the distance you'll fly for your landing at Palm Beach County Glades Airport. Make the transition to maximum cruise speed if you like.

When the OBI starts moving, it will move rather briskly. Try to time your turn (a right turn, of course) to intercept accordingly. As you roll out, PHK should be straight ahead, and you're set up for a nine-mile final to Runway 17 (the tower is nicely positioned to watch your flare and touchdown). If your gear is up, don't spoil your approach by forgetting that fact. Elevation is 24 feet.

Line Is Busy

Chart: Miami
Title: LINE BUSY PBI
En Route Coordinates:
  Aircraft: N11086, E19545
  Tower: N10743.370, E19658.265
Altitude:
  Aircraft: 1500
  Tower: 24
Heading: 159
Time: Dawn (06:00)
Special Requirements: Set Cloud Tops 8000, Bottoms 5000

Tune NAV 1 to 115.70

This flight will have some extra touches of realism. (The overcast is one of them, and notice, if you have a color monitor, how it affects the dawn lighting, making it seem more like that of a dark day, and indeed, in my opinion, more like dawn than the regular dawn.)

Our destination is a big and busy airport, Palm Beach International, West Palm Beach, Florida—about a half hour from where you are now, given an airspeed of about 120 knots.

As you fly, you'll simulate using your radio, and you'll "hear" other pilots and the PBI tower. (You'll even pass where I live and am writing this at the moment. I'll point out that hallowed ground to you from the air.)

For the purposes of this flight your aircraft identification number is N1407S. After you first identify yourself, it is abbreviated "Zero Seven Sierra."

Intermixed, below, with conversation between you and the PBI tower are just parts of typical communications between other pilots and the tower, as you would hear them during an actual flight. You are YOU, other pilots are MIX, and PBI is Palm Beach Approach Control (North). Information in brackets is me talking to you. Unpause now and read as you fly. Don't simply respond to, but do what the tower instructs you to do. But be sure it's you the tower is talking to, not somebody else. (You might even try saying your part out loud.)

You are approximately over Stuart, Florida, at St. Lucie Inlet, which you can see to the left of your course. This is the point at which pilots approaching from the north typically make first contact with the PBI tower. You are picking up your microphone and doing that now.

YOU: Palm Beach Approach, this is Cessna One Four Zero Seven Sierra.

PBI: Zero Seven Sierra, Palm Beach. [Contact established.]

YOU: Zero Seven Sierra is on the shoreline at Stuart, inbound for full-stop landing.

PBI: One Four Uncle contact Palm Beach Approach on one two five point two. He'll keep you advised on your traffic. [125.2 is Palm Beach Approach (South). Aircraft One Four Uncle has traffic: an aircraft in its vicinity that poses a potential collision hazard.]

MIX: Two five point two, One Four Uncle.

PBI: Zero Seven Sierra, squawk zero two two one.

YOU: (Setting your transponder to squawk 0221) Zero Seven Sierra squawking zero two two one.

PBI: Zero Seven Sierra, radar contact. Continue your approach. Report Jupiter Inlet. [Tower has identified you on radar.]

YOU: Report Jupiter Inlet. Zero Seven Sierra. [You will be at Jupiter Inlet when your DME reads 35.8, so keep an eye peeled.]

MIX: Palm Beach Approach, Cherokee Eight Two Five Five Alpha.

PBI: Northwest Fourteen Eighty Four contact Miami Center one three two four five. Good day. [Northwest 1484 was just passing through the PBIA airspace.]

MIX: Thirty-two forty-five now, Northwest Fourteen Eighty Four. [The "1" is sometimes dropped in repeating a frequency, since all aircraft communications frequencies begin with a 1, for example 132.45.]

PBI: Five Five Alpha, radar contact. Turn right heading two two zero.

MIX: Five Five Alpha two two zero.

PBI: Five Five Alpha descend to two thousand five hundred for vectors to the ILS, niner left. [55A will fly a practice ILS approach.]

MIX: Five Five Alpha to twenty-five hundred for vectors ILS nine left.

PBI: Four Two X-Ray, traffic twelve o'clock six miles southbound, five thousand three hundred unknown. [42X's traffic has not made contact with the tower, thus is "unknown."]

MIX: Four Two X-Ray is looking. [Looking for the "unknown."]

PBI: Five One Six, check your transponder on again please, squawk zero two four zero, and what's your destination?

MIX: Vero Beach and squawking zero two four zero.

PBI: Four Two X-Ray, traffic's passing off your right—no factor.

MIX: Four Two X-Ray. Do not have them in sight.

PBI: Roger, but he's no factor.

MIX: Palm Beach, Piedmont Seven Hundred. We're passing one point one for seven thou . . . er . . . five thousand.

PBI: Piedmont Seven Hundred, Departure Control. [Approach is also performing a Departure Control function at the moment.] Good morning. Radar contact. Climb maintain seven thousand. [Climb maintain is an abbreviation for "Climb to and maintain. . . "]

MIX: Up to seven thousand. Piedmont Seven Hundred.

PBI: Piedmont Seven Hundred turn left heading two niner zero.

MIX: Left two nine zero. Piedmont Seven Hundred.

[When you reach Jupiter Inlet, about 35.8 DME]:

YOU: Palm Beach Approach, Zero Seven Sierra is over Jupiter Inlet.

PBI: Zero Seven Sierra, roger. Say your airspeed.

YOU: [Say it.]

PBI: Zero Seven Sierra, climb maintain two thousand five hundred.

YOU: Leaving fifteen hundred for twenty five hundred. Zero Seven Sierra. [Pin down that altitude exactly. No "almost" . . . no "more or less" . . . 2500 on the nose.]

MIX: Palm Beach, this is Four Two X-Ray, leaving your area. Request disengage.

PBI: Four Two X-Ray, radar service terminated. Squawk one two zero zero frequency change approved.

MIX: Four Two X-Ray. Good day.

[When you reach 19.0 DME, you'll see Lake Worth ahead, a trifle to the right of your course. Point toward the lake, which is actually a continuation of the Intracoastal Waterway. The highway along the shoreline is U.S. 1, and the highway inland is Interstate 95. Notice the road that connects them diagonally. That road virtually points to my pad, which is in a small apartment complex on the west shore of the lake, about a mile north of the Lake Worth Inlet. The inlet should now be visible. If you don't wave as you go by, I shall definitely be offended, as will my parakeet.]

PBI: Zero Seven Sierra, report the airport in sight.
YOU: [When it is] Zero Seven Sierra has the airport.
PBI: Zero Seven Sierra, turn right heading two seven zero. Descend and maintain one thousand five hundred.
YOU: Right heading two seven zero. Descending to one thousand five hundred feet. [Well, you won't get a chance to fly directly by my place, but you can wag your wings. I'll see you.]
PBI: Zero Seven Sierra, your traffic is a banner-tower eastbound at a thousand feet. [That's a plane towing a banner, not a banner tower.]
YOU: We have no contact. Zero Seven Sierra. [You don't see him, but he's up there almost every day. He's on his way to the ocean to fly up and down the beach, towing some message or other.]
PBI: Zero Seven Sierra, report over the Turnpike. [The Turnpike? That's a new one! Well, it's Florida's Turnpike, west of I-95, and will appear momentarily off your left wingtip (you may not see it straight ahead).]
YOU: We're over the Turnpike. Zero Seven Sierra.
PBI: Zero Seven Sierra, turn left heading one eight zero. Expect landing Runway Niner Right.
YOU: Left to one eight zero. Expect niner right. Zero Seven Sierra. [09R/27L is the shortest runway at PBI, 3152 × 75.]
PBI: Zero Seven Sierra, you'll be number two behind a Cessna on a three-mile final. [Meaning another Odyssey reader must be up here! He or she will be landing ahead of you. Or are you the reader on the three-mile final? This gets confusing!)
YOU: [When Runway 09R, the short and southernmost one,

is just ahead of your left wingtip] Zero Seven Sierra, request turn final for niner right.

PBI: Zero Seven Sierra, clear to land.

YOU: Zero Seven Sierra. [IS YOUR GEAR DOWN? IS YOUR GEAR DOWN?] Phew! Then, when you're on the ground and in your landing roll:

PBI: Zero Seven Sierra, contact Ground Control on one two one point niner. Good day.

YOU: Two one point nine. Thank you. Good day.

The Road to Freeport

Chart: Miami
Title: RD TO FREEPORT
En Route Coordinates:
  Aircraft: N10807, E20106
  Tower: N10733.729, E20204.975
Altitude:
  Aircraft: 1500
  Tower: 11
Heading: 204
Time: Daylight

Unpause and follow the highway you see on the left side of your windshield. As you begin the flight, you are looking toward the aptly named town of West End on the northwestern tip of Grand Bahama Island. The highway will take you to Freeport International Airport.

Fasten your seatbelt a little tighter than usual because you're flying in the Bermuda Triangle.

Grand Bahama Island, and Great Abaco Island east of it, are the northernmost of the Bahama Islands. Grand Bahama is about 83 miles long, and Freeport is its major resort city, with a full complement of hotels and tourist and convention facilities.

While only a few of the northwestern islands in the chain are accessible to us in the simulation, the Bahama group comprises 700 limestone islands and over 2,400 rocks and cays (keys)—actually the peaks of a submerged mountain range—and numerous coral reefs. After a couple of centuries as a crown colony, the Bahamas became an independent nation in 1973.

Freeport International is on the north side of the highway, and parallels it, so if you keep the road to your right you'll be in fine position for a landing on Runway 06. Elevation is about 14 feet.

I don't know about you, but I saw some strange lightning when I was on final. And now that I've come to a stop, I'm looking at a crazy triangle of water in the sky. It merges with a lopsided rectangle of sky at the far end of the runway. If I didn't know this ugly phenomenon was almost universal at airports near water in the Amiga version, I'd blame the Bermuda Triangle.

I love airports near water, and I trust that one day soon we'll have an Amiga version without these unhappy and illusion-shattering bugs.

The Isle of Nowhere

Chart: Miami
Title: ISLE OF NOWHERE
En Route Coordinates:
    Aircraft: N10985, E20370
    Tower: ——
Altitude:
    Aircraft: 1443
    Tower: ——
Heading: 181
Time: Daylight

Maybe this island has a name, and maybe it hasn't. But as far as I'm concerned it has never been discovered, 'way out here where—as a notoriously unhumorous senator once described a forsaken place—"the hand of man has never set foot."

I came upon this little arrowhead of green island in the lonely Atlantic purely by accident (if, indeed, there are such things as accidents) and fell in love with it immediately from the air. Chances are one could fly for many years in the area of the Bahamas and never spot it. Luck was flying with me.

I vote we simulator pilots claim this gem as our own "island paradise," if you will. I call it The Isle of Nowhere, but you can give it some other name if you like.

If you start a descent and continue straight ahead, you'll discover what can be described as a perfect natural landing strip, right along the ocean. (Up to this very moment, I give you my word, I have not landed on The Isle of Nowhere; I'm going to experience it the first time, just like you. When I tell you the field elevation, below, you'll know I've set the airplane down.)

We'll regard the strip of earth ahead as Runway 18 on the Isle of Nowhere Airport, where field elevation is—in my version—precisely 13.6240 feet.

Now that we're both on the ground, I've worked out a takeoff position, usable in all versions because it involves no fractions: N10940, E20375, Heading 179. But actually, since we can assume The Isle of Nowhere is everywhere flat, we can take off and land absolutely anywhere on it. So perhaps you'll want to set up a tiedown that suits you. And, if you have Tower capability, put an observer wherever you like. It is, after all, your island, and nobody can say you nay.

By the way, you can raise both the Freeport and the Treasure Cay VORs from here, the former on a frequency of 113.20, the latter on 112.9. So civilization is well within reach.

Flamingo Fling

Chart: Miami
Title: FLAMINGO FLING
Ground Coordinates:
  Aircraft: N10783, E20833
  Tower: N10783.097, E20831.296
Altitude:
  Aircraft: 0
  Tower: 14
Heading: 297
Time: Night (01:00)
Special Requirements: This night flight requires a working knowledge of VOR navigation, and some instrument capability. See text.

You're looking at the numbers for Runway 27 at Marsh Harbour Airport, Marsh Harbour, Bahamas. And we're about to make a relatively long night flight to Nassau. I trust you won't fall asleep on me.

I hasten to tell you why we're flying over the ocean to Nassau at night: I want to spend the whole day tomorrow in that town. Sort of like a vacation. I want to see the flamingos. And I want to get a little sun on Paradise Beach. The other reason is, I think we both could use some night flying/navigating experience; you're never too good or too old to learn, and we've flown most of this book in easy daylight.

What, if anything, will we be able to see on this flight? I don't know. I'm making it for the first time, same as you. But one thing is sure: We'll be able to see the instrument panel at all times.

Speaking of which, tune your NAV to Treasure Cay, on 112.90. We're out of range for the Nassau OMNI; we'll get it later. Set the OBS to R184. It will read FROM because the station is northwest of us.

What we'll do is take off, climb out of the pattern, and then turn left heading 225 degrees to intercept R184 at an approximate 40-degree angle. As you can see from your chart, that's bound to happen before we've flown very far.

So proceed. Climb to 400 feet before you turn to your intercept heading. Plan on a cruising altitude of 2500 feet. If we can't see anything, we might as well see it from that altitude as any other I can think of. And, of course, get into maximum cruise configuration.

A couple of-roads are visible, but there's no telling where they lead.

You've only a shallow turn to make for intercept, so wait until the OBI actually moves to center.

At about 40 DME you should be able to raise the Nassau VOR on 112.70 (I'm giving you the frequency because I realize how intently you're studying the darkness out ahead.) Radial 184 should still be fine, so just fly the needle. You'll probably be slightly off the radial, and at this distance out—where the radials are far apart—you can reasonably use a 30- or 40-degree cut to get onto it.

I trust black is one of your favorite colors because there's sure a lot of it out here. You look great in black.

If you have Tower capability, continue flying but arrange for the tower at Nassau International now: N10138.120, E20747.276, accepting whatever ALT may result. Then take the Tower view. Slightly comforting to see you're right on the money, isn't it? Assuming, of course, that you are on the money.

Too bad there's no moonlight in the simulator. Wouldn't it be nice to see it shining on the water, and lighting up the edges of the rocks and cays?

I'm wondering whether there's a rotating beacon on the Nassau airport. Somehow, I doubt it. I don't think we'll see a thing until we see the runway complex.

But tomorrow I'm going to see lots of stuff. I'm taking a one-day vacation. I'm going to buy a straw hat. I'll take a ride down quaint narrow streets in a surrey with a fringe on top. And I'm going to watch the flamingo show, and check out Bluebeard's Tower. But in particular I'm going to have a swim at Paradise Beach, even though the water is too warm—like a bathtub. To get to Paradise Beach, you have to take a "bumboat" from the wharf. (As you can guess, I've been to Nassau—went there once in "real" life.)

Right now, I'm having to work to hold my altitude. How about you? For some reason, this airplane either wants to climb or descend, and I have to check every few minutes to see which it is currently trying to do.

I'm reading 17 DME and still no sign of the airport. Anyway, it's high time we consider what our approach will be.

Assuming the wind is still from the west, Runway 27 will be the active.

At about 15 DME there's a road ahead—civilization!

Nassau International is one of those late-blooming airports. But at about 12.5 DME is finally shows up.

We're close to paralleling the crosswind leg. So, considering the lateness (or earliness) of the hour and the sparseness of traffic, the tower instructs us to cross directly over the airport at 1000 feet, and then to join the downwind leg. Elevation is 10 feet. And by the way, your final will be over a very pretty though invisible lake, so caution: It would be distressing to have to swim to shore in all that darkness.

How do you think I'll look in a straw hat?

Land of Legends

Chart: Miami
Title: LAND OF LEGENDS
En Route Coordinates:
  Aircraft: N9876, E20659
  Tower: N9748.7605, E20744.050
Altitude:
  Aircraft: 1500
  Tower: 17
Heading: 152
Time: Daylight

That big island on your chart that looks like an overshoe is Andros, the largest of the Bahama Islands. And I wouldn't miss flying down its east coast to Congo Town Airport on a bet. Just proceed VFR, and follow the coastline.

Andros is one of the least-explored of the Out Islands of the Bahamas because so much of it is swampland. It's actually composed of three large islands and numerous small ones, covered in part with forests that teem with bird life. Three major waterways, North Bight, Middle Bight, and Southern Bight, separate the islands. Middle Bight, which you'll be over a few minutes into your flight, is the site of AUTEC, the Atlantic Underwater Test and Evacuation Center run by the U.S. Navy with the cooperation of Great Britain and the Bahamas government.

Tourists (Christopher Columbus is regarded as the Bahamas' first, having landed on San Salvador in 1492) enjoy ocean, lake, and river sports, and bone and deep-sea fishing outside the coral reefs.

Continue down the shoreline, and you can't miss Congo Town. First you'll see what appears to be a high rise (of all things) on the shore, and before long you'll spot the airport. Elevation is 15 feet, and Runway 10 is the active. So plan accordingly.

Miami Dodgem

Chart: Miami
Title: MIAMI DODGEM
En Route Coordinates:
   Aircraft: N10347, E19651
   Tower: ——
Altitude:
   Aircraft: 346
   Tower: ——
Heading: 094
Time: Daylight

Here's a stick-and-rudder maze of buildings to challenge all your flying skills. There are numerous routes you can take through these six buildings on Miami Beach (one is hiding behind the leftmost building you see out your windshield).

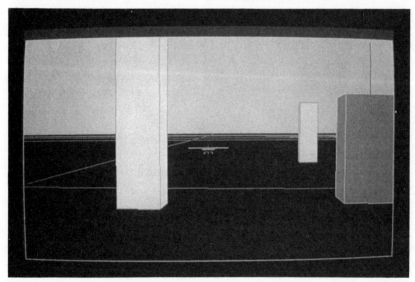

Treetop-level cruising

For starters, try flying around the left side of that leftmost building, then to the right around the building with the tower, between it and that other building—hey!—that other building!

For restarters, make up some circuits of your own from the many possibilities. And when you're finished, land on that nice strip of grass along the water north of the building complex.

Marathon Run

Chart: Miami
Title: MARATHON RUN
Ground Coordinates:
  Aircraft: N10289, E19565
  Tower: N10286.643, E19569.085
Altitude:
  Aircraft: 0
  Tower: 14
Heading: 075
Time: Daylight

In this scenario we'll depart mainland Florida, from Tamiami Airport, and head out over the Florida Keys, where we'll enjoy the interplay of blue sky, indigo water, and miles of miniature islands sparkling in the sun.

Take off on Runway 13, get your gear up, and climb straight out on the runway heading. By the time you have 1000 feet of altitude you'll see Card Sound and the beginnings of the John Pennekamp Coral Reef State Park straight ahead. Climb on up to 1500 and settle down into maximum cruise configuration.

Have a look at Miami off in the distance to your left. When you're over the Coral Reef State Park turn southward and aim straight down the Keys. Your heading will probably be within a degree or so of 207. You may see what looks like some towers or high-rises in the ocean, to the left of your course. As to what they represent, your guess is as good as mine.

John Pennekamp is actually an underwater park, popular with skin divers for its hundreds of varieties of fish and plants. Covering over 75,000 acres, it's part of the only living coral reef formation in North America.

The bright patch ahead is Key Largo, largest of all the Florida Keys. The water separating it from the mainland is called Barnes Sound. At the foot of Key Largo, U.S. Highway 1 slices over to join the island chain and become the Overseas Highway.

The Florida Keys are 135 miles long, and the 110-mile-long Overseas Highway is one of the longest overwater routes in the world. It is built on the roadbed and piers that originally supported a stretch of the Florida East Coast Railroad—a project abandoned after the hurricane of 1935. Follow the highway, keeping it right under your nose. It bears about 220 degrees along here.

Where you see the tower in the water, and where the highway jogs right and then left, is Fiesta Key. At that point you'll be 20–25 miles from our destination, Marathon Airport on Marathon Key. If you like, set a tower there at N9873.1638, E19355.881 while you fly. You'll need a good bit of ZOOM to see yourself, for a while.

Start now to keep the Keys and the Overseas Highway slightly to your left, which will make easier for you to spot the strip at Marathon.

Some of the bridges connecting the Keys are more than seven miles long, and people fish from them—as they do from piers, rowboats and charter boats. Virtually everyone in the Keys fishes.

When Marathon Airport shows up, you'll still have quite a distance to fly. When you judge you're not too far out, get into slowflight. You're cleared for a straight-in approach to Runway 25.

And what a pretty approach it is.

Airport elevation is below 14 feet.

CHAPTER FIVE
Scenery Disk 11

Tiger Field

Chart: Detroit
Title: TIGER FIELD 25
Ground Coordinates:
  Aircraft: N17448 (17448.327), E18105 (18105.815)
  Tower: N17441.101, E18097.304
Altitude:
  Aircraft: 0
  Tower: 632 (Unreliable. Change to correct if needed.)
Heading: 251 (253)
Time: Daylight

So you can make an imposing debut in Scenery Disk 11, here's your own private flying field in the heart of Detroit. We'll call it Tiger Field because you're parked opposite Tiger Stadium, visible out the right front. We also could have called it Riverside Field or Ambassador Field, because you're scenically positioned alongside the Detroit River, with the magnificently simulated Ambassador Bridge ahead of you. Behind you is the equally well-detailed Renaissance Center, the relatively new 73-story symbol of Detroit's downtown resurgence.

Detroit was founded in 1701 by Sieur Antoine de la Mothe Cadillac (Don't you love those French names?). He selected it as a center for the fur-trading industry because of its location on the strait connecting Lake Huron to the north and Lake Erie. So now you know where Cadillacs got the name Cadillac.

For a fun takeoff, fly toward some part of the Ambassador Bridge as soon as you're airborne, and buzz the roadway traffic. An observer (if you have tower capability) is on the bridge, close to the center of the span. You can climb toward his position (and for some real thrills, keep the tower view and fly in various directions around the bridge, viewing your plane with the bridge structure in the foreground.)

After you've flown a bit, shoot a landing on a heading of about 250, in the same direction as your takeoff, passing the Renaissance Center on your final.

The Crossbridge Caper

Chart: Detroit
Title: X BRIDGE CAPER
En Route Coordinates:
   Aircraft: N17438, E18096
   Tower: Same as previous
Altitude:
   Aircraft: 839
   Tower: Same as previous
Heading: 032
Time: Daylight
Note: Altitude setting may be unreliable. Your altitude should be such that you will clear the center span of the bridge. If it isn't, SLEW to a higher altitude.

    In this scenario you'll land the other way on Tiger Field. You can make the approach in one of three ways:
    1. Over The Top. Fly across the span on your present heading, then turn right and set her down.

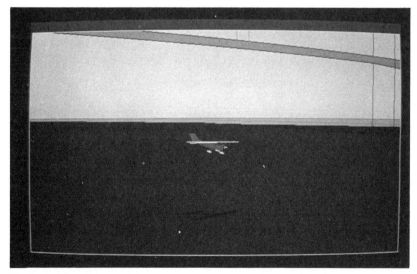

Under and over

    2. Around the End. Turn abruptly left and make an end run around the foot of the bridge for your landing (or through the opening between the leftmost towers and suspension cables).

3. Underneath. Reduce power to glide under the span, then turn right for your landing.

In all cases, your final approach should be on a heading of approximately 70 degrees. When you're on the ground, your altimeter will read about 250 feet.

The Great Glider Chases

1. Midland
Chart: Lake Huron
Title: MIDLAND GLIDER
En Route Coordinates:
    Aircraft: N18384, E19036
    Tower: ——
Altitude:
    Aircraft: 3206
    Tower: ——
Heading: 235
Time: Daylight

This and the following three scenarios will introduce you to a great new *Flight Simulator* sport—glider chasing. It's more exciting and more fun than just about anything you can do in the program, with the exception (feasible only in versions with the Tower view) of simulated radio-control flying and its associated aerobatics. Indeed, glider chasing is itself quasi-aerobatic by nature (and can involve actual aerobatics to advantage). It is more challenging and more fun than aerial combat in the World War II zone, because your "target" aircraft is three-dimensional and, up close, entirely realistic. Further, because glider chasing is so demanding of you as a pilot, it is without parallel as a training exercise. You will find yourself constantly on throttle, aileron or rudder as you wheel, then soar and dive to get into the best position. You'll do steeper turns than you thought possible, hanging on the hairy edge of stalls, changing out-the-windshield views every few seconds as you jockey your airplane around the skies . . . and all the while searching those skies for those capricious, elusive sailplanes.

The basic premise of glider chasing is this: The gliders are harmless drones, essentially insubstantial. They are pilotless, and you can crash right into and through them without damaging them or your aircraft. Thus the objective is to do just that (and do it repeatedly). Literally crash right into and through your target glider, and do that as often as possible in a given time frame.

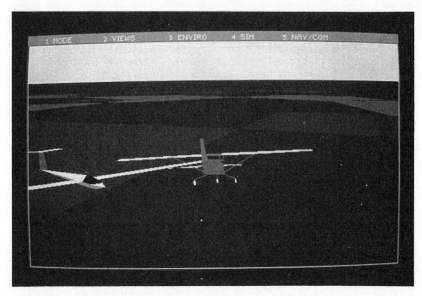

Flyers-by

This exercise is relatively easy the first time. But then the target is behind you, and before you know it's above or below you, too. And then you won't know where it is (I told you they're capricious and elusive). So the major part of your time in this simulated combat is spent looking for and then lining up with your motionless adversary. Once you have the target in your sights, are you too low or too high? If you are either of these, this calls for more power or less power, and/or elevator action. Are you too far left or right, and too low or high? This also calls for work. And if you miss this time, it all begins over again. Wow! I tell you, the only way to understand the excitement, challenge, and fun of glider chasing is to experience it. So that's what we'll do in this and the next three scenarios; there are two relatively easy ones, then two that are tougher.

In the present case, you're approaching one of the oversize gliders (I call it the Midland Glider because it's near the Midland VOR) at an approximate 45-degree angle, and a bit above *contact altitude,* which is what we'll call the optimum altitude for a *crash into and through.* The contact altitude for the Midland Glider is about 3148 feet. The simulator is not consistent in interpreting altitudes, so the parameters given cannot be guaranteed. If you don't see what the text prepares you to see in this or any glider chase scenario, adjust as required before you make a final save.

2. Ontario
Chart: Lake Huron
Title: ONTARIO GLIDER
En Route Coordinates:
   Aircraft: N18363, E19841
   Tower: ——
Altitude:
   Aircraft: 3206
   Tower: ——
Heading: 013
Time: Daylight

In this scenario you are well behind the Ontario glider (second of the oversize drones), and overtaking it. In this configuration it offers you the minimum target surface, so you may want to change your angle of attack. Contact altitude is about 3140 feet.

3. Buffalo
Chart: Detroit
Title: BUFFALO GLIDER
En Route Coordinates:
   Aircraft: N17724, E19512
   Tower: ——
Altitude:
   Aircraft: 2531
   Tower: ——
Heading: 191
Time: Daylight

This and the next glider are lifesize, thus providing far smaller targets. You and the Buffalo glider are approaching each other virtually head-on. (You may want to try a "peaceful" pass the first time, observing that this relationship makes the glider appear to be moving at high speed through the sky—check it out the rear.)
The head-on approach, like the overtaking approach,

makes a very slim target. Contact altitude is approximately your altitude at the outset, if all goes well.

4. Elmira
Chart: Detroit
Title: ELMIRA GLIDER
En Route Coordinates:
    Aircraft: N17486, E20080
    Tower: ——
Altitude:
    Aircraft: 1374
    Tower: ——
Heading: 129
Time: Daylight
Note: Again, the simulator may misread altitudes. If target is not above your altitude, SLEW up or down until it is (until the glider is visible in the sky well above the horizon).

In the Elmira situation, you are opposing the glider at an angle of less than 90 degrees, but you are below it. Contact altitude is about 2275 (in prototype scenario).

Frequently, in glider chasing, you'll have to level your wings and look out all sides of the aircraft if you hope to spot the target. When banking, it is more often than not hidden by your wing. Sometimes, on the other hand, a steep spiraling turn will reveal it with an out-the-front-windshield view.

The Road to Pembroke

Chart: Lake Huron
Title: RD PEMBROKE 17
En Route Coordinates:
  Aircraft: N19271, E19620
  Tower: N19161.218, E19760.148
Altitude:
  Aircraft: 3000
  Tower: 532
Heading: 136
Time: Daylight (Dawn/Dusk Optional)

The altitude you set and your altimeter reading may not agree. I set 3000 and my altimeter reads 3600. But no matter. With the magnificent scene before us, why quibble? Just un-pause and fly.

The river on your left is the mighty Ottawa, largest tributary of the St. Lawrence and itself father of many tributaries. It was first explored by Champlain in 1613, and for a century and a half was a great thoroughfare west from Montreal for explorers and fur traders. In the nineteenth century, lumbermen sent their immense rafts eastward to Montreal and Quebec on those waters.

This is a land of lakes, many of which merge with the river (look at it on your map). But if you follow Highway 17, it will take you unerringly to Pembroke Airport, Pembroke, Ontario, where you'll land on the runway of the same number. If, en route, you just feel like putting the airplane down somewhere alongside the river, and then taking off again, why not do that? Further, don't fly in a straight line. Turn and fly directly above the river a while, or line up to take a closer look at a lake. Fly down low over a portion of countryside, then climb again. This kind of thing keeps a cross-country flight interesting (even though this isn't a very long one.) The road will always serve to get you back on track to Pembroke, where elevation is 535 feet.

Maid of the Mist

Chart: Detroit
Title: MAID OF TH MIST
En Route Coordinates:
  Aircraft: N17935, E19339
  Tower: ——
Altitude:
  Aircraft: 500
  Tower: ——
Heading: 179
Time: Daylight

You are entering the Niagara River Canyon for one of the most engrossing rides you'll ever take—one that will tax your skills and test your judgment all the way.

You are to follow the canyon. It will not always be immediately evident which way it turns; the wrong turn will likely take you into an abstract never-never land. What should be made absolutely clear is that you must keep your altitude at about 500 feet. You'll be safe (at least as far as altitude is concerned) even down to 400 feet. But the Niagara River will swallow you and your airplane if you get much lower. This river is not at sea level. Also, you must keep as close as possible to the center of the canyon.

You'll pass under two bridges if your route is correct. As you approach the first, you'll find that the canyon walls are higher than they seemed a moment before. When the second bridge is in view, you'll know you're on the homestretch, and when you've passed under that bridge you'll know it's time to apply some power.

Water pours over Niagara Falls at the rate of 200,000 cubic feet per second, generating electric power shared by the U.S. and Canada. In your canyon flight you'll see the American Falls first, then the Horseshoe or Canadian Falls. The former are 1000 feet wide and drop 167 feet, the latter 2600 feet wide with a drop of 158 feet. The structure you see as you approach the American Falls is the 282-foot Niagara Observation Tower.

Goat Island Final

Chart: Detroit
Title: GOAT ISLAND FNL
En Route Coordinates:
  Aircraft: N17892, E19328
  Tower: ——
Altitude:
  Aircraft: 1200
  Tower: ——
Heading: 117
Time: Daylight

If you can disable Crash Detect in your version, do so for this and the following scenario, otherwise you may get a CRASH message when landing on Goat Island, or anywhere else in the vicinity of Niagara Falls. If you cannot disable Crash Detect, make the landing anyway and see if the ground supports you.

Goat Island separates the American from the Canadian Falls, just as the Niagara Canyon separates the U.S. and Canada. Here you are on final for a landing on the island, with a nice view of the falls on the way down. Elevation on Goat Island is 585 feet. When you touch down, don't be surprised if the landscape changes abruptly. There are weird effects all over the Niagara area.

Over the Mist

Chart: Detroit
Title: OVER THE MIST
En Route Coordinates:
  Aircraft: N17899, E19338
  Tower: ——
Altitude:
  Aircraft: 1154
  Tower: ——
Heading: 211
Time: Daylight
Special Requirements: See note at start of prior scenario.

This approach over Niagara Falls has you on a "sort of" base leg for Goat Island. Take off some power at the outset, so you get a good low-level view of the bridge (but remember Goat Island's elevation of 585 feet). When the landing area is proximate, bank left and set her down as nicely as possible under the tight circumstances.

Allegheny Special

Chart: Detroit
Title: ALLEGHENY SPCL
En Route Coordinates:
  Aircraft: N16648, E19348
  Tower: N16712.768, E19550.093
Altitude:
  Aircraft: 5000
  Tower: 2280
Heading: 056
Time: Daylight

Unpause immediately and fly as you read.

The altimeter (and your engine, too) may be cantankerous around here. Nevertheless, your assignment is to fly from where you are to Johnstown-Cambria Airport, Johnstown, Pennsylvania, where you'll land on Runway 09. You're to maintain at least 5000 feet of altitude until you have the airport in sight. On your right are some ranges of the Allegheny Mountains. You'll navigate by VOR, but more than that I won't disclose. This is one flight where you're entirely on your own.

You'll need to study your chart, obviously, and take a few other things into account too. I'm sure you're up to the job.

Johnstown is the site of the great and terrible flood of May 31, 1889. After extremely heavy rains, a dam across the South Fork of the Conemaugh River, 12 miles above the city, gave way and released 700 acres of water 60 to 70 feet deep. The wall of water coursed through the valley at frightening speed, and in less than an hour Johnstown was almost completely destroyed. Seven other towns in the valley were entirely wiped out. Wreckage piled up against a Pennsylvania railroad bridge, and many people clung to it to escape drowning only to face an equal horror when the wreckage caught fire. Between 2000 and 3000 lives were lost, hundreds of them never identified, and damage was estimated at $12 million. But in a remarkable demonstration of courage and vision, the city was rebuilt over the ruins of the flood (which was not the last the city was to see; it has been repeatedly devastated, most recently in 1977).

A Stop on the Underground Railroad

Chart: Detroit
Title: UNDERGROUND RR
En Route Coordinates:
    Aircraft: N17361, E18888
    Tower: N17272.897, E18876.288
Altitude:
    Aircraft: 3500
    Tower: 919
Heading: 257
Time: Daylight

You're approximately paralleling the downwind leg for Runway 08 at Ashtabula Airport, Ashtabula, Pennsylvania. But meanwhile you have a beautiful view of Lake Erie stretching—limitlessly it seems—to the horizon. And indeed it does reach from here to Toledo, Ohio, well over a hundred miles.

The highway you see on your left is Pennsylvania State Highway 11. When the near end of it is well to the rear of your left wingtip, turn left to a heading of 170 and you'll be on a long base for Ashtabula, which you'll already have seen out there. Airport elevation is 922 feet.

In Ashtabula there's a tourist attraction called Hubbard House, which was a station on the historic *underground railroad* of the days prior to the Civil War. Railroad terms such as *station, lines, conductors,* and *freight* were used to describe the various aspects of the railroad, an organized, secret system by which slaves were helped by sympathetic northerners to escape to freedom in Canada. This was in defiance of the Fugitive Slave Acts, laws passed by Congress denying runaway slaves a jury trial, and imposing severe fines or prison sentences on citizens who helped them or failed to report them. Some slaves walked from their plantations to the Ohio River, moving by night and guided by the North Star, to connect with the system. Most of the *conductors* were slaves themselves. One of them, Harriet Tubman, working with other abolitionists such as Ralph Waldo Emerson and John Brown, led more than 300 other slaves to freedom. The stations, many run by Quakers such as abolitionist Levi Coffin, *president* of the railroad (along with Robert Purvis, also a president), provided food and shelter along the way. The routes the slaves took were *lines,* and they were referred to as *freight* or *packages.* Coffin's home here in Ohio was the meeting point of three lines from Kentucky. Estimates of the total number of slaves helped to freedom by the railroad range from 40,000 to 100,-000, and its very existence represents a bright spot in American history.

Full of Hot Air

Chart: Detroit
Title: FULL OF HOT AIR
En Route Coordinates:
    Aircraft: N16652, E17685
    Tower: N16601.401, E17523.795
Altitude:
    Aircraft: 1750
    Tower: 923
Heading: 260
Time: Daylight (Dawn/Dusk too)

    In western Ohio (and proceeding by dead reckoning to
Portland Municipal, Portland, Indiana), what do you see but
that crazy thing drifting along the shoreline of Grand Lake. At
first it looks like the people in the gondola are waving at
you—sort of a friendly greeting between fellow airpersons.
But as you come closer, you realize they're waving you off.
They think you're too close for comfort.
    However, you can't resist the closest possible examina-
tion, can you?

Watch out for the balloon

As you pass by, take all your left-side views and then a rear view. Then get on a compass heading of 265 degrees. That'll take you directly to Portland Municipal for a landing on Runway 27, elevation 925 feet. There's nothing below all the way, except farmland producing corn, oats, wheat, and soybeans. But you haven't far to fly.

The Center of the World

Chart: ——
Title: CENTER OF WORLD
Coordinates:
  Aircraft: N18268, E15876
  Tower: ——
Altitude:
  Aircraft: 65000
  Tower: ——
Heading: 000
Time: Daylight

What on earth am I talking about? 65000 feet? What gives here?

Well, this isn't a flying scenario. It came about by a little break I needed from writing, so I decided to see what, if anything, was doing at North Zero, East Zero (in the simulator, you never know what you might discover). At that location, I could see nothing but ocean in all directions, so I decided to try N32767, E32767—those values being sort of germane to computer stuff. Again I saw nothing but ocean. But for no particular reason I switched on my map, and zoomed all the way out. And I saw some geography.

And the rest is history. I started SLEWing toward the geography, and things went slowly indeed, even though I poured on lots of SLEW. But I reasoned that what I was gradually approaching wasn't a specific simulated area; it was something like a map. At first, I thought it was a world map, or at least a map of the simulator world. But the farther I SLEWed the more I realized that I was looking at something which, though large, was smaller than the world.

At some point, the whole map began shifting to the right, and I decided to change from Aircraft Orientation to North Orientation so I could get a real feeling for where I was, in a map sense you understand.

Then I saw the entire U.S. clearly, and eventually I optimized the whole situation with the view you'll see now; if you turn on your map, turn on North Orientation and zoom all the way out. (Some versions have slightly less powerful zoom.)

You can see all of North America to the western tip of

Alaska, south through Mexico to Central America and the Panama Canal, north to Baffin Island and a bit beyond, and east to Newfoundland.

Some kind of geography!

I decided to put the aircraft at the highest possible altitude, and 65000 is about it (you may squeeze out a little more if you're an absolute perfectionist, but it's a cut and dry proposition).

So this is what the simulator world looks like at (on radar/map) its maximum extension, and, out the windows, from the maximum altitude you can attain. Further, you're at the approximate center of it, which is probably Bruce Artwick's desk somewhere in Illinois (just kidding; it looks to be somewhere in Wisconsin).

In truth, the views out the aircraft windows are quite breathtaking when you consider how far you're seeing. You overlook Lake Superior out the front and side, Green Bay and Lake Michigan to the right and right rear. The Mississippi River is visible out the left side and rear. You can also see the network of Interstate Highways for untold miles. The mind boggles.

Maybe we'll try this same trick when we get to Western Europe to see how far we can see. But for now—back to flying.

CHAPTER 5

Say It Isn't Soo

Chart: Lake Huron
Title: SAY IT ISNT SOO
En Route Coordinates:
  Aircraft: N19171, E17738
  Tower: N19231.280, E17567.284
Altitude:
  Aircraft: 3000
  Tower: 1690
Heading: 277
Time: Daylight

You are over the North Channel segment of Lake Huron, proceeding along the shoreline of south central Ontario, with St. Joseph Island directly to your left. The Bay Mills Indian Reservation is just beyond the sharp turn of the highway ahead to your right, and around that same corner is Lake George. As you round that corner, you'll be on the border between Ontario, Canada, and northern Michigan.

Proceed with the flight, staying over the channel and turning right where it turns. As you approach the second right turn you'll see two towers well to the right on your windshield. Turn right to a heading of about 330 degrees, with the towers to the left of your course. You'll be pointed toward a small canal, which you'll distinquish more clearly after a few minutes of flying.

Following the canal, where you see Interstate 75 crossing the water you'll be directly over the Soo Locks, between the twin cities of Sault Ste. Marie, Michigan and Sault Ste. Marie, Ontario. The Sault is pronounced *Soo* in both cases, which explains why the locks are popularly known as the *Soo Locks.*

The locks, and an artificial waterway system—the Sault Ste. Marie Canals, or Soo Canals—were created to enable ships to bypass the rapids of the St. Marys River and to link the vital water routes of the Great Lakes. The locks lift boats more than 20 feet, from the level of Lake Huron to that of Lake Superior. The whole system freezes over in winter, but still transports enough ships in warmer months to rank as one of the world's busiest.

The airport off to your left is that of Sault Ste. Marie, Michigan; but continue beyond the locks, favoring the left

126

shoreline, and the canal will lead you straight to Runway 29 at the other Soo Ste. Marie. (The *Ste.,* or course, is an abbreviation for the French Sainte, meaning Saint.) Airport elevation is a healthy 1689 feet. If you have tower capability, an observer is standing just at the runway threshold.

As you complete your landing roll, you may want to apply your brakes momentarily and change the time to dawn, dusk, or night. Then over to your right you'll see there's an operating lighthouse out on Lake Superior.

End of a Story

Chart: Detroit
Title: END OF A STORY
En Route Coordinates:
  Aircraft: N17872, E19412
  Tower: ——
Altitude:
  Aircraft: 1500
  Tower: ——
Heading: 280
Time: Daylight
Note: Although this scenario ends with a landing on Goat Island, do not disable Crash Protection even if you're able to.

This little triangular arm of water flowing into the Niagara River at North Tonawanda, New York—about 15 miles north of Buffalo—may not look like much. But it's just that, much.

This is the quiet conclusion of a story that begins many years ago and about 365 miles east of here, at Albany, New York. I am indebted to a fine businesswoman and dear friend, Shirley Levit of Florida, for suggesting its inclusion in our Odyssey.

This is the end of a historic inland water route, the Erie Canal.

As early as the 1700s, men had envisioned a waterway reaching west from the Atlantic Ocean, one that would link the Hudson River with the Great Lakes and thus the heartland of the American continent. But to realize such a dream, man would have to construct it with his hands, literally digging a path for it westward along the Mohawk Valley and the Appalachians, attempting to wrest a great, navigable ditch from what was a ruthless wilderness.

Early in the nineteenth century, federal financing for such a project was sought and denied. It was De Witt Clinton, mayor of New York City from 1803 to 1815, and unsuccessful presidential candidate opposing James Madison in 1812, who in 1817 campaigned for governorship of New York with the promise that *Clinton's Ditch* could and would be dug. He won the election and work began that year. Nine years later the fruits of a labor of epic proportions were realized . . . and not without its toll in lives.

An unbelievable engineering accomplishment for its time, replete with locks and aqueducts, the Erie Canal was all men had dreamed it would be. In 1825, a celebration in New York hailed the arrival of the initial procession of boats on the Erie Canal, and Clinton poured a keg of Lake Erie water into the Atlantic.

The canal turned Buffalo into a great port, and along its shores, towns and cities were born and thrived. It was the chief migration route for settlers of the Middle West. It turned cities like Cleveland, Detroit and Chicago—as well as New York itself—into mighty hubs of trade and finance. Farm products were shipped east along it, and manufactured products were shipped west. Other canals would soon emulate the Erie, but it was the first and greatest of them all.

With the advent of railroads, the canal lessened in importance, and was allowed to deteriorate. But early in this century it was repaired, modernized and incorporated into the New York State Barge Canal system, where today it continues to serve as an indispensable commercial route.

So that little geometric arm of water ahead of you has quite a history, though this is all of it to be found in Scenery Disk 11. Follow its lead to the Niagara, and then turn northward with the river and follow it. You'll see Niagara Falls International ahead, but pass by it and point toward the distant Niagara Observation Tower. Shoot a landing—one more time—at your private strip on Goat Island, but this time shoot from the opposite direction. Your heading on final will be about 285. Mind your landing roll doesn't carry you over the edge.

Brakes! Brakes!

Now why do you suppose that happened?

Well, those are the breaks. But it was erie—I mean eerie—wasn't it?

Lake Nipissing Getaway

Chart: Lake Huron
Title: NIPSSNG GETAWAY
Ground Coordinates:
  Aircraft: N19295, E19090
  Tower: N19284.744, E19008.990
Altitude:
  Aircraft: 0
  Tower: 1218
Heading: 291
Time: Daylight

How would you like your own vacation place on a quiet lake, surrounded by woods, far from the hubbub and harassments of daily life, with your own landing strip, and yet so close to a local airport that you could fly to this place for a picnic lunch? Hmmm?

Well, I have just the spot. I've even packed the lunch (tunafish sandwiches, what else?) Follow me.

We take off from Runway 31 at North Bay Airport, North Bay, Ontario. As soon as you've climbed to about 1500 feet, turn left to a heading of 200 degrees. There will be a highway junction ahead of you, where Highway 11 going south meets 17 which tracks the north shore of Lake Nipissing.

Climb on up to 2000 feet.

When you reach the lakeshore, follow it westward on a heading of about 295 degrees, keeping the highway well to your right. You'll see a little notch of lake not far ahead (Believe it or not we're almost there already!).

Just beyond where the highway crosses the water, there's a little triangular island in the lake. The highway crosses its northern end. Your place is at the southern end, and your landing strip is along the very edge of the water. You probably won't see it clearly until you're over the notch of water, and the geography settles down.

The lake defines the threshold and the left side of your landing strip, and you visualize the right side.

Set her down gently on a heading of about 295. Field elevation is 1220 feet.

If you don't have a good lake view after you come to a stop, taxi to one. Or set up the next scenario. Either way, we won't have the picnic until we have a nice view to go with it.

Lake Nipissing, Runway 29

Chart: Lake Huron
Title: LK NIPISSING 29
Ground Coordinates:
  Aircraft: N19285, E19008
  Tower: Same as previous
Altitude:
  Aircraft: 0
  Tower: Same as previous
Heading: 295
Time: Daylight

Anytime you're uptight, you just come here to your Lake Nipissing getaway spot and sit and contemplate the scenery. You have good views of the water out front and side, and even a transmitter tower way out there on the horizon to keep you company. Then when you feel like flying, you just fire her up, take off, and survey the scenic lakes in this area of Ontario (there are many of them to your right), as well as the shoreline of Nipissing itself. When you're ready, come back here and land, or follow the highway east to North Bay Airport.

Try approaches to your field from both directions. Landing to the east, you can think of the strip as Runway 11, bearing about 115 degrees. For a quick familiarization glimpse of that approach, put the aircraft at N19290, E18893, altitude 2000, and heading 115.

Forty-Two Ax Handles, Plus

Chart: Lake Huron
Title: 42 AX HANDLES +
En Route Coordinates:
  Aircraft: N18799, E17870
  Tower: N18639.218, E17885.148
Altitude:
  Aircraft: 2900
  Tower: 720
Heading: 188
Time: Daylight

Fly this heading toward Phelps Collins Airport, Alpena, Michigan, while I relate a little story that belongs to these parts, though certainly not exclusively.

Truth is stranger than fiction, to be sure, but legend is often larger than either of them. Our world would be poor indeed without its great myths. And one of the greatest of them is that of Paul Bunyan, mightiest of all the lumberjacks who ever were.

You are flying over northwestern Lake Huron. And possibly (just possibly) somewhere in the vastness of Ontario, behind you, the tales of Paul Bunyan first began to be told; for they may be of French-Canadian origin, among the loggers of Ontario and/or Quebec. But just as possibly they may be of American frontier origin, begun here in Michigan, or in Wisconsin, far west of you, or Minnesota, still farther west. They may have been brought here from the old country.

But wherever they began, before the start of this century the legends of Paul Bunyan had spread throughout the northwest, and when a version of them was first published in 1910, oral tradition had carried them to every corner of the country.

A bearded giant, mighty of muscle, Paul Bunyan was the ruler of American life between the Winter of the Blue Snow and the Spring That the Rain Came Up From China. Besides being a lumberjack of Herculean strength, he was a superior hunter, a great inventor, and a mighty orator.

Paul Bunyan was the Superman-like entertainment of lonely nights in logging camps. Around the fires men told of his great blue ox, Babe, who measured 42 ax handles plus a plug of chewing tobacco between the horns. The cookhouse in

132

his camp was mountainous, and you couldn't see from one end of the supper table to the other. He could cut down miles of trees with one swing of his ax. And Babe helped shape the land by drinking rivers dry.

It was Paul who carved out the Rocky Mountains, as well as Grand Canyon, and who dug Puget Sound. Perhaps—who knows?—he may have scooped out Lake Huron, too.

When Phelps Collins shows up ahead of you, you'll be in position to line up for a long final for Runway 19.

Now, this runway is the longest in the world, as well as the widest. It's 15 miles wide and 90 miles long. The whole U.S. Air Force could take off from it simultaneously, and on this day 40 years ago they did just that, in a spectacular airshow designed to bolster recruitment. They all climbed to the edge of the stratosphere and then let down and landed again straight ahead, on the same runway where they took off. Though the spectators were given special ear protectors, to the Air Force's horror, the roar of all the engines split mountains and knocked down every building within 300 miles of the airport, and the heat of those engines set Lakes Superior and Huron boiling. The turbulence from the mass flight of those aircraft is still aloft in the skies of America today, in what we know as The Jet Stream.

Steel Yourself

Chart: Detroit
Title: STEEL YOURSELF
En Route Coordinates:
   Aircraft: N16712, E19173
   Tower: ——
Altitude:
   Aircraft: 1781
   Tower: ——
Heading: 312
Time: Daylight

Ahead is downtown Pittsburgh, Pennsylvania, at the confluence of the three rivers for which Three Rivers Stadium (in Roberto Clemente Memorial Park) is named—the Monongahela (to your right), the Ohio (a continuation of the Monongahela), and the Allegheny.

The skyscrapers with which you're about to mess around mark Gateway Center, situated adjacent to Point State Park. Together they comprise the Golden Triangle of America's "Renaissance City," so-called for its rebirth from what was the dingy *steel city* of smoke and soot not many years ago, described by its own mayor as "the dirtiest slag pile in the United States." In 1980 Pittsburgh launched Renaissance II, its second improvement program since World War II.

Your mission is to fly between the two rightmost buildings, then around the left side of the third building. To accomplish this you needn't stay on your initial heading. Approach the problem any way you see fit. You may find it's a bit tougher than it looks. And like any good stunt pilot, you may want to fly over there and assess the layout of things before your first attempt.

The CN Tower, Toronto

Chart: Detroit
Title: CN TOWR TORONTO
En Route Coordinates:
  Aircraft: N18150, E19193
  Tower: N18112.815, E19204.128
Altitude:
  Aircraft: 1700
  Tower: 250
Heading: 173
Time: Daylight

Like many features in the simulator, that tower far ahead of you is sometimes fragmented as you approach it. It seems to construct and unconstruct itself regularly. But when you get closer, you'll see it's indeed substantial, as well as unusual.

This is the CN Tower in Toronto, the world's tallest free-standing structure, soaring 1815 feet high. Obviously, it's the place to be for views of Toronto. It also features a revolving restaurant, and your altitude puts you exactly at dining level, so you'll have excellent views of the bubble out the left side as you fly by.

The graphic at the outset, or at any stage of this pass, also underscores a fact worth remembering: If you're flying straight and level, you are at the altitude of any nearby vertical structure that is at the same eye-level as the horizon. Note that the bubble splits the horizon. Throughout your flight, it will be at your eye-level for ideal out-the-window viewing. Your knowledge of this horizon-sighting technique will be useful when you're flying in mountainous areas, wondering whether or not you can clear the next ridge. In other words, if a mountaintop or a building or whatever is below your visual horizon, you'll clear it. But you must be flying level (not climbing or descending) for this sighting technique to work.

Continue on to Toronto Island Airport, just ahead, and put the airplane down on Runway 15. Field elevation is 253 feet.

On the Path of the Bald Eagle

Chart: Detroit
Title: PATH/BALD EAGLE
Ground Coordinates:
  Aircraft: N16978, E19767
  Tower: N16978.054, E19766.819
Altitude:
  Aircraft: 0
  Tower: 1953
Heading: 057
Time: Daylight

What a beautiful setting for an airport!

This is Philipsburg Mid-State, Philipsburg, Pennsylvania. And it just happens to represent a perfect opportunity for putting the horizon-sighting technique (from the prior scenario) to the test. Although you're not blessed with information on your chart about mountain altitudes (in fact, mountains don't show up on your chart period), here's an example of how to check those altitudes before you even start your flight:

You're at the foot of the Appalachians. The 057 heading should have you pointed toward the peak of the ridge you'll encounter on your Runway 06 takeoff. Enable SLEW, and use it to increase your altitude until an entire, unbroken line of the horizon is just visible on the other side of the peak; at this point, freeze the SLEWing. Your altimeter now reads the altitude you need to clear the mountain—in my version, about 3040 feet.

At this point, you might as well SLEW to your right and examine the other range, just to be safe . . . and it appears that the same altitude will clear that one too.

But what was that black shape way over there to the southeast? I have a feeling, from studying my atlases, that it may be Bald Eagle Mountain. We'll soon find out.

Now SLEW down to ground level again, and then to a heading of 026. When you're there, pause, disable SLEW, and prepare for your takeoff (save the mode first if you wish).

Climb straight out at full power to about 3100 feet. Then level off and point for the peak of the ridge. As you near it, use more or less throttle, a notch or two at a time, to keep the horizon just visible over the mountain. If you do that, you may skim the treetops, but you'll clear the mountain.

It may be hard to tell when you're over the top, due to the way mountains are textured in the simulator. You'll know you're over them for sure when you see more and more of the horizon. Anyway, when you're approximately at the top, make a long, right turn to a heading of about 174 degrees. This will point you toward the approximate center of that black shape we saw when we were SLEWing earlier. Keep your altitude at or slightly above 3000, and you'll see you can clear whatever it is easily.

You're flying over Black Moshannon State Park (there's skiing here in the winter), and I have to believe the black shape is Bald Eagle Mountain. The only way we can tell for sure is get over the top of it and then look at it via the map facility. So when a straight-down view shows nothing but mountain under you, pause and enable the map view. And— what do you know?—there are two additional mountains down there.

Switch to North Orientation and set the ZOOM factor to 1.00.

No atlas I know of shows mountains really clearly—that is, dimensionally—but according to my best atlas references, those highways are U.S. 220 going northeast, and U.S. 322 going more or less east. And the big mountain is Bald Eagle, and the other two, in order, are Tussey and Jacks.

Return to your cockpit view, unpause, and let's turn to the left and fly up the valley between Bald Eagle and Tussey. In fact, start losing some altitude, point straight up the valley, and let's shoot a landing there. I don't know what the elevation is, but I'll tell you in a minute . . .

A little under 2000 feet.

I like this place! In my version the grass is dark green and the mountains are black with green outlines—quite realistic-looking for simulator mountains. Finding this was worth the trip.

But now, back to Philipsburg. However, to save you time I'll put you in the air . . . on a very interesting, and not easy, landing approach there. See the upcoming scenario.

Downwind Mountain

Chart: Detroit
Title: DWNWND MOUNTAIN
En Route Coordinates:
  Aircraft: N16992, E19752
  Tower: Same as previous
Altitude:
  Aircraft: 3000
  Tower: Same as previous
Heading: 161
Time: Daylight

Well, I didn't say we'd land on 06, whence we took off. The wind has turned around and is from about 345, so obviously our landing will be on Runway 34, for which you're presently downwind as you can see.

All you have to do is start losing altitude while continuing your downwind heading, turn base before you hit the mountain, and then turn final and touch down. Nice as you please.

Remember that airport elevation is 1956 feet.

(I suggest that, to avoid embarrassment, you slow the airplane down on the downwind leg.)

CHAPTER SIX
Western Europe

Land's End Final

Chart: Southern UK
Title: LANDS END FINAL
En Route Coordinates:
  Aircraft: N18327, E12135
  Tower: N18314.000, E12167.000
Altitude:
  Aircraft: 1500
  Tower: 282
Heading: 112
Time: Dawn (06:15)
Note: For maximum enjoyment of this scenario, be sure time
     is set to dawn as shown above before you set the N, E,
     and heading coordinates. If you see precisely where
     you're going the effect will be spoiled.

Lighthouse Ho!
And, dark as it is, Land Ho!
You've actually made it across the Atlantic Ocean to
Great Britain. But only barely. You're very low on fuel, and
could never make it to Exeter, the nearest airport. You can't
even raise the Berry Head OMNI station. No choice but to
land straight ahead on that black geography, and hope it isn't
full of rocks and ruts, or worse yet, trees. No way to guess
field elevation, either. All you can do is keep your eyes peeled
and proceed with a final at your lowest possible speed, hoping
for the best. Do not deviate from your 112-degree heading.

Fittingly, the little point where you set her down is called
Land's End. It's at the westermost tip of England. And when
you're on the ground, advance your clock an hour so the sun
rises.

Aha! It's a pretty place indeed. You might even want to
make this a landing field of your own. And that's easily done.
The tower parameters given at the head of the chapter place
you (whatever version you have) picturesquely on your Land's
End Airport, ready for takeoff.

Welcome to England!

It Really Wales

Chart: Southern UK
Title: IT REALLY WALES
En Route Coordinates:
  Aircraft: N18695, E12981
  Tower: N18739.191, E12917.187
Altitude:
  Aircraft: 1500
  Tower: 224
Heading: 305
Time: Daylight

You're on a long final over Bristol Channel to Runway 30, Cardiff Airport, Cardiff, Wales.

Wales is a part of England, and it isn't. It's a country within a country, holding fast to its own Celtic language and culture even after centuries of union with Great Britain. Cardiff has been its capital since 1955, and is a major coal shipping port. And Cardiff is sort of a city within a city; the newer Cardiff consists of parks, gardens, tree-lined streets and shopping arcades while the older Cardiff is of Cardiff Castle, which dates from the early 11th century, and on the site of which was a fort in Roman times.

And how about the Cardiff Giant?

Sorry, wrong Cardiff. The Cardiff Giant was turned up by men digging a well near Cardiff, New York, in 1869, and was exhibited around the country as either a "petrified man" or a prehistoric statue. Scientists and scholars lent serious discussion to the matter until it was revealed as a hoax. A chap named George Hall of Binghamton had taken a block of gypsum manufactured in Iowa, carved it roughly in the shape of a human figure, and buried it where the well-diggers dug it up.

Cardiff has a ramp and taxiways that are well-detailed and it's one of the five airports in England where you can refuel. Airport elevation is about 226 feet.

Avon Calling

Chart: Southern UK
Title: AVON CALLING
En Route Coordinates:
  Aircraft: N18788, E13082
  Tower: N18709.546, E13074.039
Altitude:
  Aircraft: 1900
  Tower: 625
Heading: 230
Time: Daylight

You're over the River Severn, an estuary that flows into Bristol Channel just ahead of you. And to the left of your course you'll see the Avon River, a small one as simulated, but a large one in the history of voyages.

There are two rivers named Avon in England. This one is the Lower or Bristol Avon (Bristol is the metropolitan area you can see out the left side). Where it flows into the Severn there's a town called, logically enough, Avonmouth. The other is the Upper or Shakespeare Avon, due to its proximity to Stratford-on-Avon.

Many an early voyage departed England via Bristol and that inconspicuous rivermouth down there, the most notable of them being that of John Cabot (who was not English but Italian, born Giovanni Caboto). Prior to his time, the merchants of Bristol had carried on an extensive trade with Iceland via the port.

Hired by Henry VII, Cabot sailed the Mathew and its crew of 18 men out of Bristol on May 2, 1497, in search of a western route to India. After 52 days at sea they landed at Cape Breton Island, or possibly Nova Scotia, thinking they had reached the northeast coast of Asia. On a second voyage a year later, he is believed, though he seems not to have had the vaguest notion where he was, to have reached Greenland and sailed on to Chesapeake Bay, arriving safely back at Bristol in autumn of the same year. His voyages were the basis of English claims in North America. (Think what he could have done with a few VOR stations out there!)

Continue your flight, and after you pass Avonmouth keep a lookout out the left side for the airport at Bristol. When it's

141

just ahead of your left wingtip, turn to a long final for your landing on Runway 15. Elevation is 627 feet.

There are numerous waterfront inns in Bristol, and I suggest we stop in at one of them, Llandoger Trow, for a grog. It was once a pirate den, and in *Treasure Island,* Robert Louis Stevenson made it the favorite hangout of Long John Silver.

The Chalk Giants

1. White Horse of Uffington
Chart: Southern UK
Title: UFFINGTON HORSE
En Route Coordinates:
  Aircraft: N18756, E13369
  Tower: ——
Altitude:
  Aircraft: 1060
  Tower: ——
Heading: 179
Time: Daylight

The four giant chalk figures featured in the U.K. simulation are representative of nearly 20 that are found on the English countryside. Some are from the eighteenth and nineteenth centuries, but a few are much more ancient. Little is known of any of them, except that men carved them by cutting deeply into the ground until they reached the underlying chalk surface. The ancient mythical figures may have religious significance, and the more recent ones simply may be imitative of the idea of the ancients.

The White Horse of Uffington is believed by antiquarians to date from the first century B.C., in part because its shape resembles that of horses shown on Celtic coins minted in that era. Longer than a football field, the horse stretches 360 feet across a hillside in Wessex Downs, southwest of Oxford.

If this and the other figures were not carefully tended, they would soon be overgrown and hidden by vegetation. But the local villagers keep the areas and gouges clean, and scour the chalk regularly.

In all four chalk-giant scenarios, you are positioned at the ideal altitude for studying the figures using the straight-down (ground) view from the cockpit as you fly over. Use Pause to study the figures.

2. The Whipsnade Lion
Chart: Southern UK
Title: WHIPSNADE LION
En Route Coordinates:
   Aircraft: N18817, E13655
   Tower: ——
Altitude:
   Aircraft: 1000
   Tower: ——
Heading: 086
Time: Daylight

The giant lion etching is found in the area of Whipsnade Wildpark, just across Highway M1 west of Luton Airport. When you've passed over it, you can continue straight ahead and land on Luton's Runway 08.

3. The White Horse of Westbury
Chart: Southern UK
Title: WESTBURY HORSE
En Route Coordinates:
   Aircraft: N18637, E13209
   Tower: ——
Altitude:
   Aircraft: 815
   Tower: ——
Heading: 178
Time: Daylight

This second and much more recent white horse is in Westbury, a village southeast of Bristol, at the western edge of the Salisbury Plain.

4. The Long Man of Wilmington
Chart: Southern UK
Title: WILMINGTON MAN
En Route Coordinates:
   Aircraft: N18370, E13788
   Tower: ——
Altitude:
   Aircraft: 848
   Tower: ——

Heading: 180
Time: Daylight

This is to me, at least philosophically, the most intriguing of the four figures in the simulation. The Long Man of Wilmington—Wilmington being a village east of Brighton and just north of Eastbourne on the northern coast of the English Channel—seems to be trapped in a small enclosure. Or perhaps he is simply standing in an open doorway. But to my mind the position of his arms and hands is more suggestive of entrapment. Curious.

What is this, you ask?

When you've viewed him, fly ahead to the Channel and west along the coastline to Shoreham Airport, west of Brighton. When you spot the airport, keep it to your left as you get on a heading of about 300 degrees—on a left base for a landing on Runway 21. Elevation is 7 feet.

Take Off For London

Chart: Southern UK
Title: RDY HEATHROW 10
Ground Coordinates:
    Aircraft: N18661, E13651
    Tower: N18661.132, E13651.136
Altitude:
    Aircraft: 0
    Tower: 83
Heading: 097
Time: Daylight

This scenario has you lined up for takeoff on Runway 10 Left at London's Heathrow Airport. The field is on the western outskirts of the city, and the runway heading points you straight toward the heart of things. You may want to use Heathrow as a general home airport in the area, particularly inasmuch as it has a fuel station, pilot shop, and the only ILS facility in the Southern United Kingdom simulation (10L is the ILS runway). Also, you're all set to go immediately. Taxiing around Heathrow is rather difficult, and not all that cosmetic due to its big black ramp areas—indeed, I find them rather depressing.

Heathrow is the airport of arrival for most visitors to London. Besides airline buses and taxicabs, a station of the Underground, or Tube, connects the airport with the center of the city.

Use this scenario to fly a left-hand pattern around Heathrow, and familiarize yourself with its layout, and particularly its size. Runway 10 Left is so long you'll be airborne in a little more than a tenth of its length; you'll think you're flying along a highway.

In the next group of scenarios we'll take closeup views of the major sightseeing attractions in London itself.

Ringing Big Ben

Chart: Southern UK
Title: RINGING BIG BEN
En Route Coordinates:
  Aircraft: N18663, E13733
  Tower: ——
Altitude:
  Aircraft: 260
  Tower: ——
Heading: 108
Time: Daylight

    You are directly over Kensington Gardens, at very low altitude. The swath of water is called The Serpentine. It's actually an artificial lake, on the other side of which is Hyde Park. Kensington Gardens and Hyde Park together comprise the largest public park in central London. The Serpentine is large enough for Londoners to enjoy sailing and boating on it. Not simulated is a small body of water called Round Pond, much in favor with model yachting enthusiasts.

Broad turn around the tower

Your flight path toward the Houses of Parliament will
also take you over Buckingham Palace, which in the simulation is simply a solid rectangle. The palace is, of course, where
Queen Elizabeth II lives, and the scene of the famous changing of the Queen's Guard. She must not be in residence today,
otherwise the Royal Standard would be flying above the
building.

To your right (pause when you're close to the big clock
tower, and take right side views) is Westminster Abbey,
somewhat more shapely than Buckingham Palace, though
without surface details. Actually, this is London's greatest
Gothic church, site of the coronation of English kings and
queens since the days of William the Conqueror. It was originally a Benedictine monastery. It is also the gravesite of many
renowned English poets—Browning, Chaucer, Dickens (though
he was not a poet), Dryden, Thomas Hardy, Samuel Johnson,
Kipling, Spenser and Tennyson—in the Poet's Corner. The
Tomb of the Unknown Warrior, also in the church, honors
the fallen of World War I.

The real sightseeing treat in this scenario is the Houses of
Parliament or, as it's called officially, the Palace of Westminster. Keep your altitude low and try flying just to the right of
the Big Ben tower. The clockfaces are simulated, and you can
almost see the hands.

The famous clock tower stands 315 feet high, and Big
Ben itself, whose deep-throated chimes can be heard all over
London, weighs more than 13 tons. If Parliament is in session,
a light shines in the tower at night, and a flag is flown atop it
in the daytime.

St. Paul's Cathedral?

Chart: Southern UK
Title: ST PAULS CTHDRL
En Route Coordinates:
   Aircraft: N18662, E13755
   Tower: ——
Altitude:
   Aircraft: 260
   Tower: ——
Heading: 300
Time: Daylight

All I can say is, this is approximately where one would expect to find St. Paul's Cathedral in the city of London, and according to the documentation, St. Paul's Cathedral is supposed to be simulated in the Western European Tour, and there is a building of some sort down there. But surely any other resemblance to St. Paul's Cathedral, living or dead, is purely coincidental. This building must have been digitized in one of those famous London fogs. Architect Sir Christopher Wren is probably turning over in his grave at this depiction of his baroque masterpiece, which even in this day of skyscrapers dominates the London landscape with its massive proportions and great dome, topped by a Golden Ball.

What? You don't even see a dome? Time you cleaned your glasses.

The Tower of London

Chart: Southern UK
Title: TOWER OF LONDON
En Route Coordinates:
  Aircraft: N18663, E13758
  Tower: ——
Altitude:
  Aircraft: 206
  Tower: ——
Heading: 148
Time: Daylight

The very words, "Tower of London," can inspire a towering horror in the soul. The infamous structure, just this side of the ghoulish-looking bridge named for it, is the essence of all that was medieval and monstrous.

Built originally as a fortress by William the Conqueror, it later served as a castle, but then became a prison of numerous towers, with dungeons for such famous personages as Princess Elizabeth, Sir Thomas More, Sir Walter Raleigh, and many more. Among those beheaded or otherwise murdered inside those walls were Ann Boleyn and Katharine Howard (Henry VIII's queens), Richard III's nephews (smothered on his orders) and his queen's relatives, Lady Jane Grey (briefly Queen of England in 1553) and her husband Guilford Dudley, Sir Thomas More, Sir Roger Casement, and many other of England's notables. Its last prisoner was Hitler's deputy, Rudolph Hess, who was interned here after his arrest in Britain until the 1946 Nuremburg Trials.

There's also a Jewel House in the tower complex, where the Crown Jewels are displayed under tight security, as are the Koh-i-noor Diamond and—the largest cut diamond in the world—the Star of Africa.

Just beyond the tower is, of course, the Tower Bridge, with its massive Gothic towers and thick suspension cables. Your thing will be to fly under the center section, between the towers.

Regent's Park Final

Chart: Southern UK
Title: REGNTS PK FINAL
En Route Coordinates:
   Aircraft: N18652, E13749
   Tower: ——
Altitude:
   Aircraft: 1000
   Tower: ——
Heading: 328
Time: Dawn (06:01)

There being no airport close to London, we'll create our own. And while we do that we'll have a look at the city lights—a new simulator feature inaugurated in the Western European Tour disk.

Your landing approach over the Thames gives you a great view of the Houses of Parliament and Westminster Abbey (note Kensington Gardens/Hyde Park and The Serpentine to the left of your course). The view gives you some idea of the vast London metropolitan area.

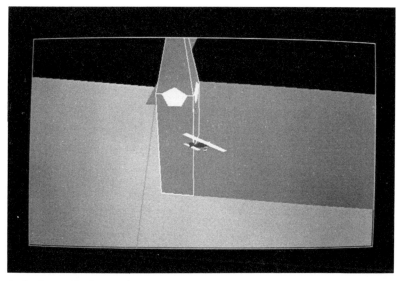

Just above Parliament

151

The patch of green directly ahead, where you'll land the airplane, is Regent's Park. First designed by famous British architect John Nash (1752–1835) as an elegant residential area, it was turned into a public park instead. It contains Queen Mary's Garden in a section called Inner Circle, but if you land on the left edge, one of two Outer Circles, you'll not trample any flowers.

The tower on your right as you descend is, I believe, the Post Office Tower named in the documentation. But it may be a quite recent addition, since I find no mention of such a tower in my references. Elevation of Regent's Park is 86 feet.

To the North Sea

Chart: Southern UK
Title: THE NORTH SEA
En Route Coordinates:
    Aircraft: N18660, E13817
    Tower: ——
Altitude:
    Aircraft: 1000
    Tower: ——
Heading: 162
Time: Daylight

It's time for some nice, peaceful flying over the English countryside or, as William Blake put it so memorably, "England's green and pleasant land."

You're well east of London, about halfway between the city and the point where the River Thames empties into the North Sea. Just follow the graceful, sinuous windings of the river.

And while we're quoting poets, you might like to be reminded of those haunting lines by Rupert Brooke in *The Soldier:*

> If I should die, think only this of me:
> That there's some corner of a foreign field
> That is for ever England. There shall be
> In that rich earth a richer dust concealed;
> A dust whom England bore, shaped, made aware,
> A body of England's, breathing English air,
> Washed by the rivers, blest by suns of home.
> And think, this heart, all evil shed away,
> A pulse in the eternal mind, no less
> Gives somewhere back the thoughts by England given.
> Her sights and sounds; dreams happy as her day;
> And laughter, learnt of friends; and gentleness,
> In hearts at peace, under an English heaven.

You have two options as you reach the North Sea. If, when the Thames begins to widen, you hug the north shore you'll spot Southend Airport, at Southend-On-Sea, and can make a straight-in approach to Runway 06 (elevation 49 feet). If you want to fly a bit farther, stay close to the south shore of the river until Manston Airport appears, and set up an approach for Runway 11. You'll be landing on the easternmost tip of southern England. Field elevation at Manston is 177 feet.

Chalk Up One

Chart: Southern UK
Title: CHALK UP ONE
En Route Coordinates:
  Aircraft: N18464, E14150
  Tower: N18404.054, E13993.838
Altitude:
  Aircraft: 1200
  Tower: 7
Heading: 255
Time: Daylight

You've just entered the Strait of Dover, with the North Sea behind you and the English Channel ahead. Off to your left you can actually see the coastline of France, in the area of Calais. And just ahead of you on the right is the coast of England, in particular, that section of coast where the famous White Cliffs of Dover are located.

Will we see any white cliffs? I don't know, but I'm determined to find out. (The cliffs are white, by the way, because actually they are chalk, and thus are more properly called Chalk Cliffs.)

We haven't far to fly, because if the chalk cliffs are simulated we should come up on them any moment, so keep an eye peeled to the right front and side.

But also, keep a watch ahead because Lydd Airport will show up on that knob of land that reaches out into the Channel. By the time you see Lydd, you'll also have seen—or noted the conspicuous absence of—the Chalk Cliffs of Dover.

Yell if you see them, but don't get so excited you mess up your landing on Lydd's Runway 22, elevation 10 feet.

To The Isle of Wight

Chart: Southern UK
Title: ISLE OF WIGHT
Ground Coordinates:
  Aircraft: N18423, E13261
  Tower: N18356.729, E13443.663 (at destination)
Altitude:
  Aircraft: 0
  Tower: 60
Heading: 038
Time: Dusk (19:00)

Your airplane is parked rear of the taxiway at the south end of Hurn Airport, in Bournemouth on the English Channel. Bournemouth is the south coast's leading beach resort.

Take a look at your chart. This evening we'll fly south to the Channel and then east along the coast. We'll track The Solent (the narrow body of water on the north side of the Isle of Wight), and then set ourselves up for a landing on Runway 30 at Bembridge Airport. Plan on your maximum cruise configuration.

Taxi ahead to the threshold of Runway 35, and proceed with your takeoff. When you've climbed to about 500 feet, do a 180 to the right, rolling out on whatever course puts a blinking light straight ahead of you. This is one of numerous lighthouse beacons along this coast.

As you fly, take some right side views of the city lights of Bournemouth. When you're over the water, take a left front view and note how The Solent lies in relation to the coast and the Isle of Wight. Turn left to head approximately over the center of it. You'll enter the passage at its narrowest point, and thereafter stay close to the north shore of the island.

Along with a couple of transmitter towers, there will be another lighthouse beacon visible off to your right. It's at St. Catherine's point, at the southern tip of the Isle of Wight.

Before long, Bembridge will show up as a bit of light to the right of your course. On the other side of The Solent the city lights of Portsmouth will turn on.

Fly to a point just beyond the northeastern tip of the island, and then turn downwind (heading 120 degrees). We'll fly a righthand pattern for Runway 30. Time to slow the airplane up and get your gear down.

When you are well beyond the runway as seen out the right side, turn base (210 degrees) and continue to execute your approach and landing. Elevation is about 63 feet.

Stonehenge: Just Passing Through

Chart: Southern UK
Title: STONEHENGE PASS
En Route Coordinates:
  Aircraft: N18570, E13245
  Tower: ——
Altitude:
  Aircraft: 86
  Tower: ——
Heading: 045
Time: Daylight

Human beings have always been intrigued by massive and immutable things from antiquity, particularly when they are cloaked in mystery. Among such oddities are the giant chalk figures we viewed earlier, the staring stone faces of Easter Island, the vast "landing strips of the gods" markings on the Nazca Plain in Peru, and the thousands of megalithic monuments found in western Europe, the Mediterranean, India, and numerous Asian countries. Among such monuments, the one ahead of you—Stonehenge on England's Salisbury Plain—is probably the most mysterious as well as the most famous.

A little terminology may be helpful. *Megalith* is from the Greek for "big stone." When a tall megalith is set upright on the earth like a pillar, it's called a *menhir,* from a Celtic dialect meaning "long stone." A group of menhirs arranged in a circle is called a *cromlech,* and a group arranged to serve as a tomb, of any size or shape, is called a *dolmen.* Perhaps the simplest of dolmens is a stone slab resting on two menhirs, forming an arch or *trilithon.*

The Stonehenge site dates from the second or third millenium B.C., and comprises four circles of stones surrounded by a ditch and embankments. The ditch is 300 feet in diameter.

According to the most recent archaeological findings, Stonehenge was created in three phases over a span of many centuries, and each phase involved transformations of the earlier work. The final phase, or Stonehenge III, consisted of (from the inside out) an Altar Stone at the center of the circle; a horseshoe-shaped arrangement of bluish stones (which geologists believe could only have come from quarries in south Wales, approximately 150 miles from here); a larger horseshoe of giant trilithons (both horseshoe shapes have their open ends facing northeast); a circle of the bluish stones (larger ones this time); a giant circle of contiguous trilithons; three rings of deep, wide holes; and four Station Stones (which form a rectangle and may have been used for astronomical sightings). Outside the circle is the massive, unhewn, 16-foot menhir called the Heel Stone.

Some of the individual stones of Stonehenge weigh more than 50 tons. So if, as is believed, the site was created by the inhabitants of Salisbury Plain, how did they manage to quarry and transport such stones, and erect this mighty monument, in those ancient times? The stones in most cases are carefully dressed and joined, with uprights tapering and sometimes convexly curved, so Stonehenge is an architectural phenomenon.

And not only how did the Salisbury folk do all this, but why? Was it a tomb, and if so for whom? Or was it an astronomical observatory? There is apparently little doubt that it was oriented according to the sun and moon. The Station Stones, used with other alignment stones, provided sightlines to points of sunrise and moonrise in midsummer and midwinter. Other of the megaliths may have been used with the rings of holes to predict eclipses (although this is the most controversial hypothesis of all). Or are the astronomical phenomena of Stonehenge purely coincidence?

Experts of one sort and another have argued Stonehenge for centuries. We may safely assume that far more is unknown about it than is known.

Although you are nominally in flight toward the Stonehenge site, you are virtually (perhaps literally) on the ground. I put you at this altitude so you could see the monument (if monument it is) silhouetted against the sky.

So why didn't I position you at a standstill right at the site? Because in the simulation, Stonehenge (as you've discovered if you've observed it closeup) is just outlines. No megaliths. Insubstantial as air. Your view while still paused, and for the first second or so of your flight, is the optimum view.

As you get closer, the illusion will evanesce. Further, you'll find you can fly right through Stonehenge without knocking over anything, and with no damage to your plane or yourself—as if, one might say, you are some kind of spirit.

Operation Dynamo

Chart: Northern France
Title: OPERATN DYNAMO
En Route Coordinates:
  Aircraft: N18410, E14413
  Tower: N18348.963, E14274.842
Altitude:
  Aircraft: 1500
  Tower: 14
Heading: 244
Time: Daylight

You are over the Strait of Dover, but along the coast of France instead of England; and here the strait is called the Pas de Calais, and the English Channel is called La Manche.

There is a historic beach just ahead, where the land sticks out its shoulder. It's that of the coastal town of Dunkirk, famous for a mass evacuation of troops, called *Operation Dynamo,* by the British Royal Navy during World War II.

Early in May 1940, Germany had invaded the Low countries, Belgium, Luxembourg, the Netherlands, and advanced through Belgium and Holland to draw the British and French forces north. Winston Churchill was named prime minister, and on May 12 made his famous "I have nothing to offer you but blood, toil, tears and sweat" broadcast. On the sixteenth, the British and French began a retreat before the rapid advances of the German Panzer Corps and Rommel's 7th Division. A few days later, the Germans captured Amiens and Abbeville on the Sommes River, completing a wide corridor to the English Channel.

On the twenty-fourth, Boulogne and Calais were under attack. The British and French, forced westward and trapped at the Channel, converged on the beaches of Dunkirk. Here they were exposed to heavy bombing and shelling, and the threat of extinction. On the twenty-ninth, launching Operation Dynamo, ships of every description—naval and civilian— together with the Royal Air Force rushed to Dunkirk to effect an emergency evacuation. In all, some 900 vessels were involved. Before the Germans reached Dunkirk, more than 388,-000 British and French troops had been removed in one of the most remarkable such exercises in history. But the evacuation was not without its costs. 80 merchant and naval ships and many smaller vessels were sunk, and 80 RAF pilots lost their lives. The operation terminated on June 2, and two days later Churchill made his most famous speech: "We shall fight on the beaches, we shall fight on the landing grounds, we shall fight in the fields and in the streets, we shall never surrender."

Your short flight will take you over the beaches and along the coast to Calais for a landing on Runway 25. Elevation is 17 feet.

The Port of Le Havre

Chart: Northern France
Title: PORT / LE HAVRE
En Route Coordinates:
  Aircraft: N17814, E13623
  Tower: N17801.475, E13668.565
Altitude:
  Aircraft: 3100
  Tower: 316
Heading: 134
Time: Daylight

The Port of Le Havre area may be at the top of my list of favorite places to fly in northern France.

You are presently over the Bay of the Seine, with the Grand Canal du Havre directly ahead. Le Havre and its commercial seaport are just at the entrance of the canal, and the airport at Octeville (Le Havre/Octeville on your chart) is visible on the left side of your windshield. Deauville's St. Gatien Airport will appear on the opposite side of the canal as you proceed with your flight.

Rather than approach Le Havre directly, stay on your 134-degree heading until the runway at Gatien just touches the right side of your windshield. When that happens, enter a 30-degree bank and a long turn to the right, rolling out on a heading of 320 degrees. You'll be on an extended right base for Runway 05 at Le Havre. Start your descent, but don't let your altitude get too low. You are quite a distance from touchdown. Do, however, work to slow the aircraft to about 60 knots, for reasons that will be clear in a moment.

Keep a check on the lie of the runway out the right front and side, and when it's visible with a 90-degree view to the right, pause a moment to read.

Judging when to make a turn from base to final, as you're about to do, is far more difficult in the simulator than in an actual aircraft, due to perspective, restricted vision, and other limitations. At an airspeed of approximately 80 knots (a typical medium-speed approach), we've seen that the turn should be started when the runway threshold is just ahead of our wingtip. But there is another general guideline, for low airspeed only, that you may find helpful.

If your airspeed is in the general vicinity of 60 knots, and you are viewing your intended runway from the base leg (at a 90-degree angle to the runway heading), wait until the runway appears almost (but not quite) straight before you start your turn; then make your bank a relatively steep one (about 30 degrees). In my experience this is somewhat more reliable (but only at low airspeed) than starting the turn to final when the intended runway is just ahead of your wingtip. It seems to compensate somewhat for your slow airspeed. The runway will sometimes be almost under rather than just ahead of your wing as in a turn at an airspeed of, say, 80 knots. If on the other hand your airspeed is near the higher figure, use the just-ahead-of-the-wingtip technique. And in any case, tailor these or any methods to suit your individual flying techniques. The key thing, once you've found a technique that seems to suit you, is to be consistent.

Go ahead now with your approach over Grand Canal du Havre, and if your airspeed is around 60 knots, try the almost-straight-on view technique. Elevation at Le Havre is about 319 feet.

Operation Overlord

Chart: Northern France
Title: OPERATN OVRLORD
En Route Coordinates:
　Aircraft: N18036, E13347
　Tower: N17674.893, E13495.066
Altitude:
　Aircraft: 5000
　Tower: 260
Heading: 184
Time: Daylight

If it's possible for airspace to be historic (and why not?) then you are in historic airspace now. For in the early morning hours of June 6, 1944, there were 10,000 airplanes in the skies you are in at this moment, all pointed toward the beaches ahead of you. Below you in the English Channel and on the Bay of the Seine—stretching from here to Le Havre, about 100 miles to the east—there were 4000 invasion ships and 600 warships, manned with 176,000 Allied troops. And two U.S. airborne divisions had already landed a few hours earlier.

For this was the scene of D-Day, the day of the invasion of France, code-named *Operation Overlord.*

Technically, Operation Overlord began five days earlier, when the BBC transmitted a coded warning to the French Resistance that an invasion was imminent. The planned invasion was postponed two days because of bad flying weather.

Utah Beach, directly ahead of you, and Omaha Beach (which you'll fly over presently) are two of a series of beaches along the coast of Normandy, and the sites of the major landings. By the end of the day, 150,000 troops, thousands of vehicles, and tons of supplies had been moved ashore in the largest invasion in history. On June 10 the troops from Utah and Omaha beaches joined forces to form a solid line against the Germans, whose six infantry divisions had failed to stop the first assault.

Unpause and add some power to hold your altitude, then begin to transition to your maximum cruise configuration.

The land visible to your right and out the right front is the Cotentin peninsula, at the tip of which is Cherbourg. A

165

major transatlantic port, Cherbourg represents the western extremity of the Normandy invasion. On nearby Roule Mountain (Mont Roule) is the Museum of the War and Liberation, which depicts the invasion and the war in photographs, weapons, and equipment displays, and samples of propaganda.

As you near shore, you'll see a little notch in the geography straight ahead. There may be a lighthouse visible in the water this side of it (sometimes, in the simulation, a lighthouse will be "caught" with the light on, even in the daytime). On this side of the notch is the aforementioned Utah Beach. The highway is Highway 13, which goes from Cherbourg to the outskirts of Paris and, via other names, on into the city.

When all of the shoreline except the notch has disappeared under you, turn left to a heading of about 112 degrees so you're approximately paralleling the coast. You'll see an arrowhead of land. A very long stretch of shoreline from the arrowhead east has the G.I. name Omaha Beach. On Omaha Beach on D-Day a thousand American soldiers gave their lives. I relate that sorrowfully. If by any chance a soldier or airman or sailor or anyone who experienced Operation Overlord is also experiencing this *Odyssey,* I salute your heroism and your guts. (Happier to report is that of the 10,000 aircraft involved over the beaches of Normandy; only one was shot down—maybe one of World War II's most amazing statistics, if not the most amazing.)

Now, if your chart were accurate, you could tune the Caen VOR on a frequency of 114.50, center the OBI, and fly the indicated radial for a landing on Caen's Carpiquet Airport. As an alternative (and for a more precise approach since we'll sit the airplane down on Runway 13), you could (if you took your chart's accuracy for granted) set Radial 130 on the OBS, turn left heading about 100 degrees until intercept (the needle centered), then turn right to head 130, tracking the needle for a straight-in approach. Unfortunately, however, while the chart depicts the Caen VOR as being directly on the airport, it isn't; it is instead about 9 miles distant. The VOR technique will get you within sight of Caen, but to make things easy on yourself, simply follow the highway. Stay on the right side of it and you can't miss.

Elevation at Caen is 263 feet. Don't forget your landing checklist.

Le Mans Entrant

Chart: Northern France
Title: LE MANS ENTRANT
En Route Coordinates:
  Aircraft: N17134, E13605
  Tower: N17126.768, E13608.210
Altitude:
  Aircraft: 1000
  Tower: 194
Heading: 165
Time: Daylight

The Le Mans Circuit-Automobile, where the famous Le Mans auto race is held each June, isn't simulated, but if it were you could see the roadway over there on the other side of Arnage Airport.

Le Mans is known for more than auto racing. Founded by the Romans in the third century, it was seized in turn by William the Conqueror, by Philip Augustus, by John II who ceded it to Queen Berengaria, queen of Richard the Lion-Hearted (she is buried in its Cathedral of St. Julien du Mans), and by various others through the centuries. It was besieged during the Hundred Years' War (1337–1453), and again by the Huguenots in 1562. It was also the scene of France's defeat by Prussia in 1870–71.

But Le Mans survived all that, a civil war, and two world wars to become a modern industrial city and the capital of the Sarthe Department (departments in France are something akin to counties in the U.S.).

In this scenario you are on a special leg of the airport traffic pattern—the downwind entry leg. This is the formal way to enter a pattern on approaching an airport. The downwind entry heading is calculated by subtracting 45 degrees from the downwind heading if in a left-hand pattern, and adding 45 to the downwind heading if in a right-hand pattern. The obvious reason for entering at a 45-degree angle is so you can see, and be seen by, other aircraft that may be in the pattern. In the present situation, your landing will be on Runway 03, the reciprocal of which (the downwind heading) is 210 degrees. Once you join the downwind leg, you'll then proceed to turn base (heading 120 degrees) and then final, heading, of course, 30 degrees.

When do you turn downwind from the entry leg? The answer is right now, when your intended landing point (the threshold of the active runway) is at the approximate vertical center of your windshield. If you fly much farther, you'll be too close to the strip when downwind. So unpause and immediately negotiate a right turn to 210 degrees. Then take a 90-degree view to your left, and the runway should be readily visible while you parallel it.

Pattern flying is by no means easy in the simulator, primarily because of your restricted visibility and the lack of three-dimensional references. So don't be surprised if you mess up. It takes lots of practice before you'll develop any kind of consistency. You'll find it much easier if you slow the airplane to about 60 knots (in the present instance, on the downwind leg).

Elevation at Le Mans/Arnage is about 200 feet.

Speaking of vertical references, if I had to choose just one feature I'd like to see added to *Flight Simulator,* it would be three-dimensional references—vertical and otherwise—on airports. Think how great it would be to see a tree or so, a telephone pole or two, a couple of other planes on the taxiways and ramps, and the control tower itself (as at Livermore Municipal in California, the only structure of its kind in all the simulator world), when you're on final. Another plane for example, holding short of the active runway (which runway could be decided within the program based on wind direction), would alone give us a much-needed visual reference as to our approach altitude, and to the relative width and length of the strip. Some trees or telephone poles near the runways would do the same, in addition to making the landings (and takeoffs) far more realistic.

The Lone Eagle

Chart: Northern France
Title: THE LONE EAGLE
En Route Coordinates:
  Aircraft: N17461, E14238
  Tower: N17471.608, E14296.936
Altitude:
  Aircraft: 3100
  Tower: 221
Heading: 080
Time: Night (21:45)

Of course, we must enter Paris under something like the conditions in which Charles Lindbergh (or Lindy or Lucky Lindy or The Lone Eagle) entered it on that famous day and year, or more properly, night and year, May 21, 1927. It was then that he completed the world's first non-stop solo transatlantic flight.

Imagine, if you can, that you're in the cockpit, not of your Cessna or Piper, but of The Spirit of St. Louis. That being the case, you can see nothing ahead because your aircraft is equipped only with side windows; you'd have to stick your head out of one of them, or yaw the airplane left or right, to see Le Bourget Airport out there just below the horizon.

You've been flying for more than 33 hours since yesterday morning, when you coaxed your overloaded airplane out of the mud and into the air at Roosevelt Field, Long Island— barely missing some telephone lines as your wheels finally left the ground and you started to climb. At one point in your long solo flight you fell asleep, awaking with a jolt just in time to avoid ditching in a rough Atlantic Ocean.

According to *The Twentieth Century, An Almanac,* "Lindbergh covers the 3600 miles in 33½ hours. His flight is tracked by millions, and when he lands at Orly Airport, 100,000 people are on hand to greet him." If that was the case, of course, there'd have been 100,000 disappointed people, since he landed at Le Bourget, not Orly, at 10 p.m. Paris time.

So, just before you unpause, set your clock to about 21:-55. You should touch down on Runway 08, Le Bourget's shortest, at or close to 22:00 hours. Elevation is 224 feet.

Don't be surprised if a sea of people engulfs you and the airplane as you finish the landing roll.

There is more to the Lindbergh story than his history-making flight. Born February 4, 1902, in Detroit, Michigan, he grew up in Little Falls, Minnesota, studied engineering for three semesters at the University of Wisconsin, enrolled in a flying school in Lincoln, Nebraska, and in 1924 enlisted as a flying cadet in what was then the air service division of the War Department. He did stints with the Missouri National Guard and was a captain in the Officers Reserve Corps. In April of 1925 he became an airmail pilot on the St. Louis-Chicago route, and it was while flying the mails that he decided to compete for a $25,000 prize offered by Raymond B. Orteig for a non-stop New York- Paris flight.

In St. Louis, Lindbergh convinced a group of businessmen to finance the construction of an aircraft for the transatlantic attempt (which is how it came to be called The Spirit of St. Louis).

After the flight, he was awarded the French Cross of the Legion Of Honor, the British Royal Air Force Cross and, in the U.S. the Distinguished Flying Cross and Congressional medal. A national hero, he made an air tour of 78 cities and every state in the union. He also flew non-stop from Washington, D.C. to Mexico City in December of 1927, then to Central America, South America, and the West Indies.

In 1929 he married Anne Morrow, and their first child was named Charles Augustus Lindbergh after his famous father. The kidnapping of this son in 1932, at the age of 19 months, made world-wide headlines. The child was taken from the Lindbergh home in Hopewell, New Jersey. A note demanding a ransom of $50,000 was received, and was paid according to the instructions, but Charles Jr. was not returned. He was found dead. Four years later, in 1936, Bruno Richard Hauptman, who had been discovered in possession of some of the ransom money a few months after the murder, was convicted of the crime and electrocuted. Until the end, Hauptman would declare he was innocent.

Publicity surrounding the crime forced the Lindberghs to live in England from 1935 to 1939. Soon after their return Lindbergh resigned his Air Corps Reserve commission, under fire from President Franklin D. Roosevelt for his opposition to the proposed American intervention in World War II. An isolationist, he joined the America First Committee in April of 1941, but later the same year volunteered his services to the Air Force, and flew on combat missions as a consultant. He showed USAF bomber pilots his old time techniques for leaning the mixture of gas and air in their engines, so as to extract the maximum from their fuel on long distance flights. The results amazed the young fliers.

In 1953, Lindbergh received the Pulitzer Prize for his book, *The Spirit of St. Louis,* and a year later was made a Brigadier General in the Air Force Reserve. He died in 1974, having exemplified the sobriquet, *The Lone Eagle,* throughout all of his life.

The Arc de Triomphe

Chart: Northern France
Title: ARC DE TRIOMPHE
En Route Coordinates:
  Aircraft: N17436, E14261
  Tower: ——
Altitude:
  Aircraft: 600
  Tower: ——
Heading: 286
Time: Daylight

You are pointed toward the Place Charles de Gaulle and its centerpiece, the Arc de Triomphe. The avenue on your left is the wide and handsome Champs Élysées, one of the world's most beautiful and fashionable streets.

The Arc de Triomphe was planned by Napoleon to commemorate the successes of his armies. Actual construction took place between 1806 and 1836. The monument stands 162 feet high and is 147 feet wide.

Under the vault of the arch is France's Tomb of the Unknown Soldier of World War I, topped by the Eternal Flame. The design was inspired by Roman triumphal arches and includes reliefs celebrating Napoleon's victories. A dozen wide, tree-lined streets radiate from the Place Charles de Gaulle, and the top of the Arc de Triomphe provides a sweeping view of them.

You can fly so as to keep the monument to your left or right, taking side views as pass by. Or, you can attempt to fly through the arch. Take your choice, but in any event watch your altitude because the Place Charles de Gaulle is about 545 feet above sea level.

Montmartre Hill

Chart: Northern France
Title: MONTMARTRE HILL
En Route Coordinates:
  Aircraft: N17438, E14268
  Tower: ——
Altitude:
  Aircraft: 1000
  Tower: ——
Heading: 011
Time: Daylight

You are flying toward the Montmartre district of Paris, named for the graceful little mountain you see just ahead. Also just ahead is the most conspicuous feature of Montmartre—a brilliant white basilica named Sacré Coeur. A *basilica* was originally a type of large public building in ancient Rome, having an oblong interior divided by two rows of columns into a central area or nave and two side aisles. The basilica pattern was adapted as a basic design for Christian churches from the time of Constantine (c280–337 A.D.). The Basilique du Sacré Coeur, built after the Franco-Prussian war, is a Paris landmark visible from everywhere in the city. Fly just to the left of it and take views out the right side.

Sights on the Seine

Chart: Northern France
Title: SIGHTS ON SEINE
En Route Coordinates:
  Aircraft: N17406, E14286
  Tower: ——
Altitude:
  Aircraft: 1000
  Tower: ——
Heading: 329
Time: Daylight

Many of the notable landmarks of Paris are along the
Seine River. Here you are on the southeastern outskirts of the
city, approximately opposite the big Bois de Vincennes park,
which is skirted by both a railroad and the Rue de Paris. The
Bois de Vincennes, visible out the right side of your aircraft,
is a forest park and contains Paris' largest zoo. Inside the park,
though not visible in the simulation, is the Château de Vincennes. Now a museum, in the past it has been, by turns, a
residence for royalty, a prison, a World War II headquarters,
and, during the German Occupation, a torture chamber.

Stay at medium speed and track the river, staying more
or less over the right side of it. Numerous boulevards, which
encircle Paris in ever-narrowing embraces, cross the river
along your route. It is these boulevards that make Paris virtually round in shape. The city was designed by Baron Hauss-
mann (for whom an avenue is named) in the 1800s, and
planned so expertly that it handles even today's heavy traffic
very effectively.

Well to the left of your course is the Montparnasse District, situated on a low hill (the hill is not simulated, but the
Montparnasse Tower, visible to the left of the Eiffel Tower,
marks the area). In Montparnasse are the remains of the eerie
subterranean cemetery called the Catacombs, with dark, twist-
ing passages lined with high pilings of crossed bones and
skulls. The French Underground used the site as a headquarters during World War II. You'd need a flashlight to find your
way in there.

Just this side of where the Seine turns left you'll see a
representation of a famous botanical garden, Les Jardins des

Plantes, boasting 10,000 species of plants. Just about there, too, the famous Left Bank section of Paris—with its intermingling population of artists, writers and students—begins. You may wonder, as I did, *left* in relation to what? But I found out. The Left Bank is the south side of the Seine, and is called that because it would be to your left if you were facing in the same direction as the river flows. In this scenario, you are facing in that direction. The Left Bank will be to your left all the way from here to the Eiffel Tower.

Start losing a couple of hundred feet of altitude before the river turns left (but don't get lower than 700 feet). Just at the bend is a small island, Île St. Louis, and beyond that another island, Île de La Cité. These islands form the very heart of what was the ancient city of Paris. The city was founded there more than 2000 years ago.

Stay over the right branch of the river. You'll see a massive building on the second island. Fly to the right of it and pause frequently to admire it. This is the Cathedral of Notre Dame—the most renowned building in Paris and perhaps the most beautiful church in the world. It is handsomely represented in the simulation, although reasonably enough its flying buttresses are not shown. This is the site of Victor Hugo's gripping 1831 novel, *The Hunchback of Notre Dame* (originally called *Nôtre Dame de Paris),* and of the classic motion picture version starring Charles Laughton. In the story, Quasimodo, the cathedral's hunchbacked bellringer, kidnaps a beautiful Spanish dancer, Esmeralda, at the direction of Archdeacon Frollo. When Esmeralda is accused of a crime actually committed by Frollo, Quasimodo tries to provide sanctuary for her in the cathedral tower. Ultimately Esmeralda is taken from Notre Dame and executed by hanging, whereupon the unhappy and lovesick though unloved Quasimodo hurls the Archdeacon to his death from the cathedral.

Start gaining some altitude again as you leave Nôtre Dame de Paris behind. Immediately ahead is the expansive Palais du Louvre and the Tuileries Gardens. Keep climbing and fly directly over, rather than alongside, the Louvre, pausing wherever you like. Note the long semi V- or U-shape of the construction. Formerly one of the world's largest royal palaces, the Louvre today is one of the world's foremost museums, particularly famous for its Museum of Paintings, which includes the celebrated Mona Lisa by Leonardo da

Vinci. Among many famous sculptures in the Louvre are the Venus de Milo.

Leaving the Tuileries Gardens you'll be flying toward Place de la Concorde. Its tall, thin obelisk, visible in the simulation, was given to Charles X by Mohammed Ali in 1829, to symbolize harmony and peace, as does the square itself with its fountains and monuments. The Concorde was not, however, always so peaceful. During the French Revolution, this was where the infamous guillotine showed its ominous silhouette against the sky. Don't risk a thumbs-down gesture as you fly by.

Further along the Champs Élysées you'll spot the Arc de Triomphe, which we've already seen. So follow the Seine around to the left. And there you'll see what is perhaps the most striking feature of the Paris simulation, as well as one of the world's most famous landmarks: the Eiffel Tower. Try to fly just to the right of it on this first pass, and meanwhile start a climb to an altitude of 1500 feet. Then do a 180 and fly close to the tower again. You'll be able to see the very top with most of your views.

Beer Hall Putsch

Chart: Southern West Germany
Title: BEERHALL PUTSCH
En Route Coordinates:
  Aircraft: N17028, E16828
  Tower: N16987.542, E16853.039
Altitude:
  Aircraft: 3500
  Tower: 1816
Heading: 166
Time: Daylight

You're on a long left base for Runway 07 at Neubiberg Airport, Munich. It was in Munich's ironically festive beer hall, Hofbrauhaus, that an obscure Adolf Hitler in 1920 announced his 25-point program of German nationalism, anti-Semitism, and—because it made peace with the Allies—hatred for the Berlin government. Perhaps six persons (the other enrollees in the German Workers' Party) heard his harangue.

After serving as a corporal in the German army in World War I, Hitler in 1921 was made president of the new National Socialist (Nazi) party. Almost immediately he formed the again ironically-named "Gymnastic and Sports Division," which actually comprised his earliest storm troopers and was used to terrorize his political opponents.

Also in Munich in 1923, Hitler tried to seize the Bavarian government in an abortive Beer Hall Putsch. He was sentenced to five years imprisonment, but served less than nine months. During his imprisonment he dictated to Rudolph Hess his *Mein Kampf*, which he published in 1925.

We'll see more of Munich, closer up, in coming scenarios. But for now proceed on your base leg configuration. Elevation at Neubiberg is 1818 feet. Slow down and start losing some altitude as you fly over the city. Figure to have an altitude of about 2500 feet when you turn for your long final approach.

The Frauenkirche

Chart: Southern West Germany
Title: FRAUENKIRCHE
En Route Coordinates:
  Aircraft: N17015, E16837
  Tower: ——
Altitude:
  Aircraft: 2226
  Tower: ——
Heading: 110
Time: Daylight

The focus of attraction on Munich's skyline is the massive, twin-towered Cathedral of Frauenkirche. It was severely damaged in World War II, but has since been restored.

Just beyond the church are a group of buildings that began as a fortress, and once housed Bavarian rulers. Called simply *Residenz,* it has been carefully reconstructed following its virtual destruction in World War II. Inside are numerous sections, including a treasury of jewels, a museum containing the original palace furnishings, and a rococo theater in which Mozart conducted his musical works. In another theater, operas are still performed today.

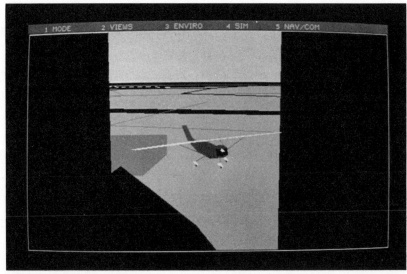

Right through the middle . . .

Alongside Residenz is the *Hofgarten,* a small park. Beyond that you can see just a bit of a much more spacious park, *Englischer Garten,* or the English Garden, a romantic place with a hilltop temple, a Chinese pagoda, pleasant paths among trees and flowers, a lake for swans, and an open-air restaurant. You can see the expanse of the English Garden out the left side before you unpause.

If you like, make one pass at Frauenkirche just for viewing, and then another in which you lose some altitude and try to squeeze between the towers. (Rest assured there's plenty of room to accommodate your wingspan. I know because it says so right here.)

Islands of the Isar

Chart: Southern West Germany
Title: ISLANDS OF ISAR
En Route Coordinates:
   Aircraft: N17021, E16847
   Tower: ——
Altitude:
   Aircraft: 2072
   Tower: ——
Heading: 203
Time: Daylight

This scenario has you flying south alongside Englischer Garten over the relatively narrow Isar River that threads through Munich. Slow up the airplane as soon as you unpause.

As you track the river you'll come up on two islands. The first is small and, at least in the simulation, of little interest. But on the second, called *Isarinsel* (Isar Island) is the giant Deutsches Museum, one of the foremost scientific and technological museums in the world. Make a low pass over it, but don't get below 1900 feet. Then for some real fun, see the next two scenarios.

Museum Piece 23

Chart: Southern West Germany
Title: MUSEUM PIECE 23
Ground Coordinates:
  Aircraft: N17012, E16843
  Tower: N17011.140, E16842.109
Altitude:
  Aircraft: 0
  Tower: 1816
Heading: 232
Time: Daylight

Many times in *Odyssey* I've tried to position the aircraft in really dramatic places, but have usually been frustrated by the inability of some versions to set fractional parameters. And it didn't seem fair to give some pilots exciting things to do in exciting places, if all pilots couldn't share in the fun.

But here's a scenario that everyone can enjoy. In fact, I'll be so bold as to say I think this is the best "improvised" simulator flying field I've come up with yet.

You are on a narrow strip of grass alongside the Deutsches Museum. (If you have tower capability, don't fail to take the observer view of your position and location. The watcher is up at the other end of the strip, just at the corner of the building; and while I'm bragging, I might as well say this is the best observer view I've ever come up with, too.)

You'll have trouble trying to make a normal takeoff here. Although the grass extends beyond the museum wall, this is an island, and on a normal takeoff run you'll charge into the Isar River before you get to flying speed.

What's called for is your best short-field takeoff. That's tantamount to saying you should take off trimmed as you would be for slowflight—or slower. I recommend you hold the brakes on while you advance your throttle to the wall, then release them when you have full rpm. Use flaps or not, depending on your favorite short-takeoff technique. Given the preceding cautions, you can take off from Museum Field handily. If you don't make it the first time, resurrect yourself and try again with a different configuration.

(If tower-view capable, let the observer watch your takeoff. You'll see you don't scrape the museum wall, though it does look awfully close—and is.)

Once you've got the takeoff mastered, don't miss the next scenario.

Landingisching?

Chart: Southern West Germany
Title: LANDINGISCHING?
En Route Coordinates:
  Aircraft: N17016, E16847
  Tower: Same as previous
Altitude:
  Aircraft: 2072
  Tower: Same as previous
Heading: 231
Time: Daylight

Well of course that nice Museum Field is of no use to you if you can't land as well as take off there. So now you're shooting a landing there.

If you don't do so well, your aircraft may wind up as a special *Americanischer Nutzisch* exhibit in the technology wing . . . after the U.S. Embassy takes care of the reparations to Munich for the hole you left in the wall (and makes the other arrangements, of course).

Olympic Event

Chart: Southern West Germany
Title: OLYMPIC EVENT
En Route Coordinates:
  Aircraft: N17053, E16895
  Tower: ——
Altitude:
  Aircraft: 2500
  Tower: ——
Heading: 255
Time: Daylight

    Northeast of Munich and aimed toward the Olympic Grounds, you're over a relatively wide body of water named Lake Dono. I confess that I named it Lake Dono because I don't know what its name is, if it has one (in my one atlas where it shows up, it is nameless). In any event, it's a wide section of the Isar River, and provides a picturesque approach to the Olympic Grounds and the great shish kebab of the Olympiaturm Tower—which is, at the outset of your flight, just a vertical line that's almost straight ahead on your windshield. Like many features of the simulator, the tower takes itself apart and puts itself together again as you approach. You'll see why I compare it to a shish kebab when you're up close.

    When you've passed over the park, turn left to a heading of 160 degrees and you'll be paralleling a long base leg for either of Munich's airports—Munich (far to your left) or Neubiberg (visible ahead). Each has a single strip, 07/25, so take your choice.

    The Olympic Games, by the way, began in 776 B.C. in Greece, in honor of the Olympian god Zeus. The Games were held every four years then, and are still held every four years today. In early times, women were not allowed to compete, nor were they in modern times—until 1912. In fact, they weren't permitted even to watch the events. So they formed their own games, called the Heraea.

    The modern Summer Games began in Athens in 1896, and the Winter Games began in France in 1924. The Games were suspended during the two World Wars.

    The modern Olympics were originally intended to recognize individual excellence, as well as promote a spirit of international goodwill. But they have become increasingly political. In 1936, Adolf Hitler refused to congratulate the great American athlete and winner of four gold medals, Jesse Owens, because he was black. In 1972 the Games were held here in Munich, but were turned into a horror when 11 Israeli athletes and coaches were murdered by Arab terrorists. The African nations boycotted the 1976 Games, and Taiwan withdrew from them. The U.S. and various other western countries boycotted the 1980 Summer Games in Moscow to protest the Russian invasion of Afghanistan. And, the 1988 Summer Games were under such threat that host South Korea, prepared special strategic SWAT-like teams to discourage and, if necessary, deflect terrorism.

Nuremberg Try

Chart: Southern West Germany
Title: NUREMBERG TRY
En Route Coordinates:
  Aircraft: N17553, E16674
  Tower: N17563.760, E16696.167
Altitude:
  Aircraft: 1750
  Tower: 1053
Heading: 070
Time: Daylight

Imagine that you're very low on fuel as you fly past the Fernmeldeturm Tower and toward the Pegnitz River that flows through Nuremberg. You take some glances at the tower (another Shish Kebab) as you go by, but you continue straight ahead, looking for a place to set your airplane down.

The only possibility, you figure, is one of those parks that skirt the water up ahead. But as you fly along, nothing looks very promising.

Then, as the transmitter tower disappears off to your left, you see it. Straight ahead. A little strip of grass on this side of the river, just beyond that quasi-circular section of roadway, and this side of what appears to be a bridge. That's your best (possibly your only) chance, but you have to work to get into position, and you'll have to estimate the field elevation as you descend.

Or is the other side of the bridge a better possibility? As you approach, you figure either stretch of grass will do—the key thing being that you don't brush with the bridge. (The tower observer is on the first stretch.)

Guten lucken!

Nuremberg is, of course, famous as the scene of the 1945–49 trials of German military leaders, as well as of judges and other civilians. Three kinds of crime were involved: Crimes Against Peace, specifically the planning and waging of aggressive war; War Crimes, the murder and mistreatment of civilians and prisoners, killing of hostages, plunder and destruction of communities and property; and Crimes Against Humanity, the extermination or enslavement of civilian populations on political, racial, or religious grounds.

An international military tribunal established by the U.S.,
Britain, France, and the USSR tried two dozen Nazis for
crimes against humanity, 12 of whom were sentenced to
death, and the rest imprisoned. Among those sentenced to
death were Hermann Goering, Joachim von Ribbentrop, and
Alfred Rosenberg. The Nuremberg trials established major
new principles in international law, the most important being
that individuals are responsible for their own acts. Today it is
regarded—at least in international law—as correct to disobey
the order of a superior if by obeying it you would commit a
crime of the type described above.

On a lighter note, Nuremberg several centuries ago was
the home of a cobbler named Hans Sachs (1494–1576), who
had a talent for comic verse. He specialized in a then-popular
type of poetic song named *Meistersang,* based on minstrel tradi-
tions. And it was this real person, Hans Sachs, whom German
composer Richard Wagner (1813–83) immortalized in his
opera, *Die Meistersinger von Nurnberg,* completed in 1867. While
outwardly the work was a comedy, Wagner himself wrote of
". . . under the opera's quaint superficies of popular humor,
the profound melancholy, the lament, the cry of distress of
poetry in chains. . . ."

The Main Frankfurter

Chart: Southern West Germany
Title: FRANKFURT-MAIN
En Route Coordinates:
    Aircraft: N17794, E15986
    Tower: N17800.156, E15986.986
Altitude:
    Aircraft: 741
    Tower: 368
Heading: 049
Time: Daylight

Talk about big airports. This is Europe's biggest and busiest, situated a short distance southwest of the city of Frankfurt Am Main ("am Main" signifying that it's on the Main River).

Since the Emperor Charlemagne held a historic *synod* (council of churches and church officials) here in 794, Frankfurt has been a bastion of liberalism and culture. It is one of Germany's major transportation hubs as well as a primary inland port.

A bevy of runways

One of the greatest German writers and thinkers, Johann Wolfgang von Goethe (1749–1832), was born in Frankfurt. Best known for his famous work *Faust,* Goethe during his 83 years of life was, besides a great author, a lawyer, botanist, zoologist, politician, physicist, painter, and more.

The philosopher Arthur Schopenhauer (1788–1860), though not born in Frankfurt, spent the later years of his life here.

Every fall a Book Fair is held in the city, attended by publishers from all over the world. And this is fitting, since Johann Gutenberg, the inventor of printing using movable type fonts, established a print shop here in 1454. The famous Gutenberg Bible—the first Bible printed with movable type—was given to the world about a year later.

Your heading has you pointed for the skyline buildings of Frankfurt, at low altitude. The Main airport tower controllers don't appreciate what you're doing. After you've crossed the field, yaw a bit to your left so as to pass just to the right of that big Fernmeldeturm TV tower. The city itself will be off to your right, but we'll have a closer look at it in the next scenarios.

After you fly by the tower, turn right to a southerly heading, aiming toward the first building that shows up ahead of you. Lose a little altitude, getting down to about 450 feet. Fly toward the building, planning to veer to the left of it at the last minute. But when you're close to it, pause a moment and admire the classic lines of the Frankfurt Cathedral (Dom). Twenty-three Holy Roman emperors and kings were elected here.

Flying beyond the cathedral, turn right to a heading of about 230 degrees and climb to 1500 feet. On the way up you should be able to spot Main Airport again, more or less straight ahead of you. When you do, plan to land on the shortest strip, Runway 18, at the far end of the field. The best approach from here is to get on a long left base while you are still a distance out. That means a heading of you-figure-it-out. Elevation is 371 feet.

Night in the Mountains

Chart: Southern West Germany
Title: NGHT IN THE MTS
En Route Coordinates:
  Aircraft: N17064, E15548
  Tower: N17191.249, E15737.850
Altitude:
  Aircraft: 2500
  Tower: 507
Heading: 030
Time: Dawn (06:00)

    Although it appears on your Southern West Germany chart, the city of Strasbourg, for whose Entzheim Airport you are ultimately destined in this scenario, is in the Alsace-Lorraine area of France.

    The mountains you are about to fly between and around are more realistic in nondaytime than most simulator mountains, which is why I chose for you to fly this scenario in the dawn's early light. Once you've flown it in these conditions, try it in the daylight, too. It's a very scenic flight.

    Unpause and make the transition to maximum cruise configuration.

    As you know from our earlier experimentation, the mountains on either side of your aircraft are higher than your present altitude. But that's no problem, since we're going up the valley.

    Point for the area ahead where the mountains almost, but not quite, appear to come together. Very shortly, you'll discover that what appears to be a single mountain on your right is actually two. If you look up the valley between them (out the right side) you'll see that there's a highway over there—so you aren't that far from civilization. Presently, you see that there is a highway ahead of you as well.

    When you judge that you can clear the last slope of the mountain on your right, fly around it, ultimately getting on a due east heading. Then very shortly—lo and behold!—the airport at Entzheim.

    Your landing will be on Runway 05, which you are approaching at an approximate 40-degree angle. So this is a good time to practice "sighting" an oblique approach (though you could simply parallel a base leg and then turn final).

But first, since the elevation at Entzheim is about 510 feet, start a gradual descent. And, because the airport is in sight, get into approach configuration (slow down).

A good suggestion (in the simulator) for judging where to start your turn to final when on a diagonal approach with the airport visible on your windshield, is this:

When the runway appears nearly straight, or is about to disappear from your windshield, start your turn, using an approximate 30-degree bank.

As with all other such approach suggestions (they're not *rules*), this one depends on your airspeed (ideally about 60 KIAS), the steepness of your bank, and other factors related to your personal flying technique, including when you start to roll out and how smartly you roll out. So let practice and its concomitant—experience—be your guide in applying the suggestion.

Across the Rhine

Chart: Southern West Germany
Title: ACRSS THE RHINE
En Route Coordinates:
  Aircraft: N17158, E15777
  Tower: Same as previous
Altitude:
  Aircraft: 2000
  Tower: Same as previous
Heading: 353
Time: Daylight

Again you're in West Germany, but in a moment, as soon as you cross the Rhine River, you'll be in France, continuing your flight toward the city of Strasbourg.

The cities in the Alsace-Lorraine area are in some ways more Germanic than Gallic. Most of the customs are those of the other side of the Rhine, including the way folks dress, the food specialties, and even the architecture.

But Strasbourg is noted for some specialties strictly Alsatian— notably its *pâté de foie gras* and other Alsatian culinary delights. Further, Strasbourg was the site where "La Marseillaise," the French national anthem, was composed in 1792— and you can't get much more French than that.

Strasbourg also has its own Notre Dame Cathedral, with a highly unusual astronomical clock. At noon, a human figure representing Death springs to life and strikes the hour, whereupon a figure representing Christ appears and blesses his Apostles. Finally, a cock crows as a reminder that St. Peter thrice denied he knew Christ on the eve of the crucifixion. That clock and all its complex workings was constructed and installed in 1574.

Your flyover will give you a good view of Strasbourg's parks, thoroughfares, and numerous bridges and canals, but there are no buildings simulated, and—thankfully—no TV tower can be found (if there were one, I'd take care not to point it out to you).

When you've left the city behind, bank left until Runway 23 at Entzheim Airport is straight ahead of you and proceed with a landing.

Lake of Constance

Chart: Uncharted
Title: LAKE CONSTANCE
En Route Coordinates:
  Aircraft: N16805, E16087
  Tower: N16810.858, E16254.483
Altitude:
  Aircraft: 3000
  Tower: 1369
Heading: 068
Time: Daylight

I don't know about you, but I'm just in the mood for a
"Lake of Constance." As soon as you've set up the parameters, go ahead and fly.

You and your airplane are on the border of Switzerland,
about 30 miles northeast of Zurich, and tracking the southern
shoreline of one of the prettiest little lakes in Europe. In the
local language it's *Bodensee* (*see* means lake), and in my various
references its both "Lake Constance" and "Lake of Constance." At the moment, I'll accept Lake of Constance.

If you check your map and zoom out far enough to see
the whole waterscape, you'll find it's shaped sort of like a
goldfish, with you at the tail-end. If you're in a hurry, you
can transition to a higher speed, but I'm going to stay in our
en route configuration. I like the interplay of water, sky, and
light-and-dark landscape. And for once I even like the utterly
flat horizon. But if I could put one cloud out there, low in the
sky, I'd reach out and do it.

Follow the lakeshore around to the right. It's hard to tell
whether those land tips touch, dividing the lake into two
parts, or simply come very close together. I think it depends
on how much rain has fallen lately.

Stay approximately over the center of the main section of
the lake.

This scenario demonstrates again what is so true of *Flight
Simulator.* You never know what you may discover. This lake
isn't shown on the Enlarged Section Southern West Germany
chart. There may be an unenlarged chart where it does appear,
but at this writing the only charts I know of are of the enlarged variety. I found this lake when I decided to have a look

at Friedrichshafen, listed in the Airport Directory. The reason neither the airport nor Lake of Constance show up on the chart is that they are both well south of Stuttgart and Strasbourg and thus of the chart extremities.

Friedrichshafen is on the north shore of the lake. If you haven't discovered that already, you will in a few moments. You can land immediately on 06 there, or fly the short distance to the tip of the lake, then do a 180 and follow the north shore back to the airport. Which you do depends on your mood. I'm sure you can guess from my tone what I'll do.

Elevation at Friedrichshafen (when you need to know) is 1372 feet.

I must share with you a bit of trivia I discovered about this little town, population 53,000. It was once the home of two unusual aircraft: the Zeppelin blimp, and the Dornier seaplane. (As I say, you never know.)

Schmed Square

Chart: Uncharted
Title: SCHMED SQUARE
En Route Coordinates:
   Aircraft: N21433, E22796
   Tower: N21434.854, E22799.764
Altitude:
   Aircraft: 309
   Tower: 83
Heading: 087
Time: Daylight

Red Square, Schmed Square—you're on your way to a landing right inside Kremlin Park. And you've picked your spot: that little stretch of grass you can see on the other side of the Kremlin wall. You'll show 'em how American pilots fly!

Or will you?

After all, you don't even know the elevation, do you? And just how far is it to that opposite wall?

However, you are committed.

So—*Glasnost!*—here goes nothin'.

Only Way Out

Chart: None
Title: ONLY WAY OUT
Ground Coordinates:
    Aircraft: N21435, E22800
    Tower: Same as previous
Altitude:
    Aircraft: 0
    Tower: Same as previous
Heading: 268
Time: Daylight

Well, the Muscovites were certainly nice to you. No harangue. No arrest. No threats. All smiles, followed by a tour of Moscow—and even a dinner complete with vodka and caviar.

But now it's the next day, and how do you get your airplane out of here?

You're looking at the answer, straight ahead. You go out the same way you came in, but in the opposite direction. If you can just make it over the wall—if you can just—then you'll be able to see the Kremlin from the air, plus Red Square (wonder who won the contest), and all that good stuff. Anyway, you really haven't a choice. This is the only way to go.

I'll just sit back and enjoy your takeoff. I have no advice to give you, and no cautions to expound. We've flown so long together now, I have absolute confidence in you. (And I won't spoil that generous compliment by mentioning that this airplane is equipped, fortuitously, with dual controls.)

Far Away Places

1. The Big Picture
Chart: None
Title: THE BIG PICTURE
Coordinates:
　Aircraft: N20178, E13252
　Tower: ——
Altitude:
　Aircraft: 1800
　Tower: ——
Heading: 360
Time: Daylight

When we were in the U.S. we took a view of the world from somewhere in Illinois. And I said when we got to Western Europe, we'd try the same thing. And this is it (though not the only such view possible).

After you set the parameters, zoom out on your map until you see Iceland—looking like a drop of paint high above the British Isles and west of the Scandinavian countries. Depending on your zoom capability, one factor shy of full zoom may give you the best view (Full zoom in the Amiga and Atari ST puts a stripe down the left side of the screen).

Here you view an expanse of Europe from the Barents Sea off the coast of Russia (and a big chunk of that country), south to the Black Sea and Turkey, east to Spain and on its eastern edge Portugal (including much of the Mediterranean and the Strait of Gibralter, with even a fringe of Algeria at the bottom of the screen), and as we've seen, north past the British Isles to Iceland.

Between Iceland and Scandinavia is the Norwegian Sea, which east of the British Isles becomes the North Sea, connecting with the Atlantic Ocean via the English Channel. The ocean above Spain and off the west coast of France is called the Bay of Biscay, but it's still the Atlantic Ocean. West of Spain you see the islands of Corsica and Sardinia, and the water between there and Italy is called the Tyrrhenian Sea. The boot of Italy is kicking the island of Sicily. To the right of this action is the Ionian Sea, to the north of which the Adriatic separates Italy from Yugoslavia, Albania, and Greece, which juts into the Mediterranean. The sea between Greece and Turkey is the Aegean, which mates through the tiny Bosporus strait with the Black Sea.

And that's the end of the geography lesson for today. (I wish I could remember it myself, but I know I won't be able to.) Anyway, anytime either of us feels like getting reoriented to this part of the world, we can refer to The Big Picture.

Now come along with me and we'll visit some areas that really aren't simulated, in the sense of being charted, documented, or featuring any detail, but are nonetheless there. We'll see that these areas, though relatively barren, are true to their real shapes, and even have the now familiar patches of light and dark landscape to relieve the monotony. In a sense, we'll be previewing things to come in the simulator—sort of pioneering where the future lies. And in another sense, we'll be flying to some parts of the world as they were in the past, before there were highways and airports and cathedrals and TV towers to see. We can even imagine—and quite easily— that we are the very first human beings to set foot on these remote lands, let alone to set an airplane down on them.

2. Reykjavik, Iceland
Chart: None
Title: REYKJAVIK,ICLND
En Route Coordinates:
  Aircraft: N25158, E10558
  Tower: N25152.315, E10603.132
Altitude:
  Aircraft: 2000
  Tower: 297
Heading: 088
Time: Daylight

You are pointed to the approximate location of what is today (you might be approaching yesterday of course) the city of Reykjavik, the capital of Iceland. This country is just south of the Arctic Circle. It was (or will be) settled by Norwegians in the ninth and tenth centuries, with an economy dominated by its fishing industry. Its people have the highest literacy rate in the world, at 99.9 percent.

Just this side of where the two land masses create a corner with the water (the land may be dark green there, looking almost like a runway, if you have a color monitor) is your intended landing point. Elevation is 300 feet.

3. Strait to Tangier

Chart: None
Title: STRAIT TANGIER
En Route Coordinates:
   Aircraft: N12483, E10908
   Tower: N12398.651, E10803.249
Altitude:
   Aircraft: 3000
   Tower: 83
Heading: 219
Time: Daylight

You're in southern Spain, looking across the Strait of Gibraltar toward your landing spot in Tangier, on the northern tip of Morocco. (How do you like that for world travelin'?)

This flight will take a little while, so you might as well get in maximum cruise configuration. When you get to the other side of the strait, regard the shoreline as your runway threshold. Elevation down there is about 86 feet.

4. Greek to Us

Chart: None
Title: GREEK TO US
En Route Coordinates:
   Aircraft: N13144, E20918
   Tower: N13121.117, E20953.932
Altitude:
   Aircraft: 3000
   Tower: 14
Heading: 140
Time: Daylight

Is that a runway ahead? And if not, why not?

You are on approach for what may become—sometime in the future—Runway 14 at Athens Airport, Athens, Greece. At the present time, however, even the Parthenon has yet to be constructed, so you're an early arriver indeed. Elevation is 17 feet.

5. Adriatic Vistas
Chart: None
Title: ADRIATIC VISTAS
En Route Coordinates:
  Aircraft: N13812, E19167
  Tower: ——
Altitude:
  Aircraft: 1835
  Tower: ——
Heading: 305
Time: Daylight

Sometimes, when you're flying this simulator, you can really believe in what you see. By luck or chance, land and water and sky merge into a picture for which you have no words. And, like clouds, the light and the shapes change moment to moment—the last moment gone forever, the next unknown. But thanks to the simple act called SAVE we can capture the best moments, and go back to relive them when the mood strikes us.

For such going back, I give you sunny southern Italy, about at Brindisi, along the shores of the Adriatic Sea.

I won't tell you where to fly now, or how far, or where to land. Like the pilots of early days, you can wing where your instincts point or your mindset dictates. As long as there's fuel sloshing around in your tanks, there's no telling where your imagination can take you, or how long it might take to get where you want to be. Too, at the last, you can set your airplane down anywhere that strikes your fancy in that remarkable world below you, like old-time pilots used to land on farms and meadows and cornfields, on strips of deserted beaches, or on roadside fields where maybe they spotted a gas station so they could fill her up.

This is, after all, your airplane. Those are your resplendent wings out there. When you unpause and fly, your engine lends its lyrical baritone accompaniment to your very heartbeat. If you listen carefully, you can hear voices in its rich pistons and in its throaty, muffled explosions, far-out voices talking to you, saying:

Your airplane, your wings, your world.

Good flying, my friend.

APPENDIX A
Basic Flying Guide

Your primary *Flight Simulator* instruments are the three round instruments along the top left of your instrument panel. By using just those instruments you can control your airplane knowledgeably and precisely—in overcast, in pitch blackness, or in bright daylight.

In all versions of the program these instruments are, reading left to right, the **airspeed indicator,** the **artificial horizon,** and the **altimeter.**

The **airspeed indicator** tells you your rate of speed through the air in KIAS (Knots Indicated AirSpeed), via a system that measures the pressure of the relative wind against your wings.

The **artificial horizon** depicts your aircraft's attitude in relation to the earth's horizon. Your wings are represented by the two longer lines at the center of the instrument, the dot between them symbolizing the aircraft's nose. In no or poor visibility, the artificial horizon is like a miniature representation of what you would see out the windshield if you could see earth and sky. It operates on the gyroscopic principle, and is sometimes called the *gyro* horizon.

The **altimeter** tells you your MSL (Mean Sea Level) altitude, your altitude above sea level, not AGL (Above Ground Level) altitude. The altimeter works by reading atmospheric pressure, which decreases as altitude increases and vice versa.

In straight and level flight, these three instruments will be virtually steady because your airspeed will be virtually constant, the aircraft's wings and nose will be aligned with the horizon (real or artificial), and you will neither be gaining nor losing altitude.

Airspeed Variations

Your airspeed indicator should vary little in the course of a well-executed flight, unless and until you change it by trimming your elevator up to a higher position or down to a lower position.

The functions of throttle and elevator must be well understood. Increasing your throttle setting does not make the airplane fly faster, and decreasing it does not make the airplane fly slower. Further, we do not make a practice of climbing by application of up elevator, nor of descending by application of down elevator.

The throttle is your *altitude* control. If you want to climb, increase your throttle setting a few notches; if you want to descend, decrease it. If you want to make the airplane stay at a given altitude, but it's climbing or descending slightly, counteract that tendency with small throttle adjustments. Altitude slipping down? Add a notch of power. Gaining altitude slightly? Take off a notch of power.

Elevator is essentially your *airspeed* control. A high elevator setting (elevator way up) will result in a slow airplane. Lower settings (settings closer to straight or neutral) will result in increasingly higher airspeeds (see "Controlling Airspeed" in Chapter 1). A straight or neutral elevator will, at normal cruising altitudes, yield maximum cruise speed. An elevator setting below neutral will pitch the nose of the aircraft down, and will only be used deliberately and briefly if at all (to recover from a stall, or to pick up speed for a steep climb as in stunting, for example). In order to fly level, neither climbing nor descending, the higher your elevator setting the less power you'll require, whereas elevator settings closer to neutral call for more power.

A light plane can be successfully taken off, flown, and landed without touching the elevator. You should try this because it will prove to you once and for all that throttle controls your altitude. Here's a way to do it:

Flying without Elevator

Set your elevator so the elevator position indicator is about three-quarters of the way up the gauge. Apply full power, and let the airplane take itself off and climb (leave the gear down). As it climbs, gradually reduce power while watching the VSI (Vertical Speed Indicator), which tells you your rate of climb in hundreds of feet per minute (FPM). Stop reducing power when you are climbing at 500 FPM (a standard climb rate). Note your airspeed (it will be relatively low due to your high elevator setting).

Climb to about 1000 feet, then further reduce power until the VSI shows a zero rate-of-climb. Adjust power up or down a notch as needed to keep the VSI needle at 0 (always give the airplane a little time to react to new power settings). With VSI 0, you'll be flying straight and level. Note your relatively low rpm reading, and that your airspeed is virtually the same as it was when you were climbing. This is cruise configuration for your particular elevator setting.

Adjust power to increase rpm by about 200, and again pay attention to your VSI. The airplane climbs.

Reduce power by about 200 rpm. The airplane again flies straight and level, but at the new altitude. Throttle is your altitude control. (If your new altitude is significantly higher than your original altitude, it will take a bit more power to fly level; adjust throttle accordingly.)

Now use aileron or rudder to turn the aircraft toward any likely landing area—anywhere there's grass and no obstruction. (If you are new to the simulator, first pause and read "Making Turns" below.)

Reduce power gradually until the VSI shows you are descending at about 500 FPM. This is the standard descent rate. With your high elevator setting, your glide is virtually flat and you can let the airplane land itself exactly as it's configured now. It won't even bounce. To stretch the glide, land further ahead. You can add a little power and the rate of descent will lessen. You could also back off your power completely, to idle, and the airplane will land safely. Note that your airspeed will remain virtually constant in any and all of these configurations. And you haven't touched your elevator at any time in the flight. Thus it is evident that, just as throttle is your altitude control, elevator is your airspeed control. Now you know it.

Making Turns

I recommend using the keyboard yoke, in preference to joystick or mouse, when that's possible (it isn't in the Macintosh version). I also recommend disabling auto-coordination, which will give you rudder control independent of aileron.

Your aileron is controlled by three keys (see your manual). They permit you to apply left or right aileron, and to center or neutralize aileron. Rudder (left and right) is controlled by two additional keys. On the ground, the rudder keys steer the nosewheel. The same key that centers aileron centers your rudder.

On the ground, use your rudder to steer, centering the nosewheel when you're pointed where you want to go.

In the air, rudder is valuable for "yawing" the aircraft (rotating it on its vertical axis; also called the yaw axis) to a slightly different heading. As a general rule, use a few strokes of rudder for a heading change of 30 degrees or less. On landing approaches, rudder will help you line up more precisely.

Ailerons are used to bank the aircraft in the direction you wish to turn. The steeper the bank, the faster the turn. You control the steepness of the bank by arresting it with the centering or neutralizing key. The sequence for, say, a left turn, is left aileron, bank to desired angle, neutralize. Then, to roll out of the left turn, right aileron, wait for wings almost level, neutralize. If the wings are not then level, get them level using small increments of aileron in the same manner.

Uncompensated banks and turns—steep ones in particular—result in a loss of altitude. The steeper the turn the more altitude loss. To prevent this, compensate for the loss of lift by adding a little up elevator before starting the turn (or even during it). As you level the wings, return the elevator to its prior position. Adding power before the turn will yield much the same result, but is usually the technique of choice for exceedingly steep turns (they may require elevator back pressure as well as higher power).

The Purposes of Flaps
Flaps are airfoils on the trailing edge of the wing. In normal flight they are at 0, and act simply as part of the wing. When extended the minimum (10 degrees) for takeoff, they increase the aircraft's lift-to-drag ratio and thus shorten the takeoff run (zero them when airborne). In flight, flaps can be used to further slow down an already slow airplane (do not apply them when in maximum cruise configuration, as the relative wind could tear them off) by increasing drag and at the same time lowering the speed at which the aircraft will stall. Finally, on landing, flaps permit a steeper angle of descent without undue increase in airspeed, and a landing at lower airspeed. Pilots frequently extend them all the way when on final approach to a runway.

The Effects of Altitude
Higher altitudes call for higher power settings (rpms), in order to deal with increasingly thinner air—the propeller has less to

bite into. Thus a power setting that finds you straight and level at, say, 1500 feet will find you descending if you're at 4500 feet. You'll need more power up there; but at the same time your airspeed will be higher. At very high altitudes, all the power you have may not be enough. When that's the case, use a higher elevator setting (spare your engine by setting your elevator high enough to fly level with something less than full power).

At very low altitudes, the reverse is the case—you'll need a lower power setting to fly level at 500 feet than at 2000 feet, and your airspeed will be lower at the lower altitude.

Runway Numbers

Runways are numbered from 01 to 36, and describe the approximate magnetic bearing of the runway to the nearest 10 degrees, with the final 0 dropped. Thus Runway 01 can be expected to bear 010 degrees or close to that, Runway 10 to bear 100 degrees or close, and Runway 36 to bear 360 degrees (equivalent to 000) or within a few degrees of that heading.

A full description of a given strip thus involves two numbers, each being the reciprocal of the other, such as Runway 06/24. Landing on 06 (which bears approximately 060 degrees), your landing is to the northeast, and landing on 24 (bearing approximately 240) it's to the southwest.

Using the OMNI

You can navigate to and from virtually everywhere in the simulator world by flying the VOR (Very high frequency Omnidirectional Range) radials. These are magnetic course radials that extend in all directions from the VOR stations that are shown, surrounded by compass roses, on your chart. The radials can be visualized as spokes of a wheel, all of which converge at a hub—the VOR station.

In the simplest case, you tune (on your NAV1 radio) the frequency of the station toward which you wish to fly. You then center the CDI (Course Deviation Indicator) or needle on your OBI (Omni-Bearing Indicator) with a TO reading, and the most direct heading to the station can be read at the top of the instrument, while your DME will tell you your distance from the station. You then turn the aircraft to that heading and proceed to fly the needle—which means keep the CDI (needle) centered at all times. If the CDI moves to the left of center, you correct a bit to the left until the needle is again at center. You then resume the heading that agrees with the radial. Keeping the needle centered may require a consistent heading that's a few degrees different than the radial number. You accept that (it's due to wind direction and other factors), and persist in keeping the needle centered.

Close to the station, the needle will deviate considerably and its movements should be disregarded. If the VOR station is on your destination airport, flying the needle will take you straight to that airport. If it's at an intermediate location, as when you're flying by means of more than one station, tune the next station as soon as you think you may be in range of it, and again center the CDI and fly the needle to the new station. If your final VOR station is not directly on an airport, fly the needle and watch for your airport where you expect to see it relative to the position of the station.

Often you can plan your flight to track a radial that agrees with the runway on which you intend to land, thus giving yourself a handy straight-in approach.

Landing Tips
Everyone who flies *Flight Simulator*—including commercial airline pilots when they first encounter it—has difficulty landing well, due largely to the absence of vertical and/or dimensional references, the absence of natural, real-world peripheral vision, and the impossibility of judging one's height over the ground (and over the runway itself) during the final approach. Only much practice will lessen the landing difficulty, and no landing will ever be routine.

But the following techniques can help you improve your landings early in the game:

1. Slow the airplane down (in the case of propeller-driven aircraft, to something between 60-80 knots). It is far easier to land a slow airplane than a fast one.

2. Give yourself some distance. Plan your flight as you near the airport, to allow yourself a reasonably long final approach. That gives you time to recognize the lie of the active runway, and to make alignment corrections early on. If you're flying a pattern, extend the downwind leg, which results in a wide base leg, and a longer final.

3. Adjust power and control surfaces (ailerons, rudder, elevator, flaps) to get and keep the runway threshold straight ahead and, most importantly, steady at a point just a little below the center of your windshield. Power is the key here

(along with flaps as desired to steepen your descent). If the runway threshold is above the visual center of your windshield, you are undershooting, such that if you continue without correction you will land short of the threshold. If the threshold is well below the center of your windshield, you are likely overshooting, and will land too far up the runway (or beyond the end of it). Remember that if something is unmoving on your windshield, you are headed straight for it. That's why you want to keep the runway threshold as motionless as possible while you descend. If it moves up the windshield, add power and/or a notch of up elevator to reduce your rate of descent. If it moves down your windshield, reduce power, put on some flaps or more rarely, add a notch of down elevator to increase your rate of descent.

The final stages of the normal landing (not all landings are normal) involve three actions:

1. Flattening the glide by means of up elevator, which further slows the airplane; done while you still have 50–100 feet to descend, depending on your relationship to the intended landing point.

2. Flaring (pitching the nose of the aircraft up) a few feet above the runway, which typically involves two quick notches of up elevator.

3. Continuing back pressure (deliberate slow notches of up elevator) until the wheels touch down. This action keeps the nose high, and in a good landing your aircraft will virtually stall at the moment of touchdown. (Should you get a stall warning before the wheels touch, use a notch of down elevator to counteract it.)

For more comprehensive study of VOR navigation, and other aspects of flight, see the author's *Flight Simulator Co-pilot* or, for the 68000 computers, *Flying Flight Simulator,* both from Microsoft Press.

40 Great Flight Simulator Adventures and *40 More Great Flight Simulator Adventures* (both from COMPUTE! Books) and *Runway USA* (Microsoft Press, contents specific to the early Scenery Disks, 1–6) offer additional flight instruction and experience. Note that only *Flying Flight Simulator* is specific (in terms of instructional content) to the 68000 versions but, if you know how to fly, some scenarios in all books can be enjoyed regardless of simulator version. *Runway USA,* for example, features numerous flights in the San Francisco Bay area.

APPENDIX B
Index to Flights